D1006587

The
Story
of Tea

The Story of Tea

OTHER LOTUS TITLES

ANIL K. JAGGIA	
SAURABH SHUKLA	*IC 814: Hijacked! The Inside Story*
ARJAN SINGH	*Arjan Singh's Tiger Book*
CLAUDIA PRECKEL	*Begums of Bhopal*
DHANANJAYA SINGH	*The House of Marwar*
E. JAIWANT PAUL	*'By My Sword and Shield'*
GERALDINE FORBES (ed.)	*The Memoirs of Dr. Haimabati Sen*
INDIRA MENON	*The Madras Quartet*
IRADJ AMINI	*Koh-i-noor*
J.C. WADHAWAN	*Manto Naama*
JOHN LALL	*Begam Samru*
JYOTI JAFA	*Really, Your Highness!*
KHUSHWANT SINGH	*Kipling's India*
KANWALBIR PUSHPENDRA	
SINGH	*The Ruse*
K.M. GEORGE	*The Best of Thakazhi Sivasankara Pillai*
LAKSHMI SUBRAMANIAN	*Medieval Seafarers*
MANOHAR MALGONKAR	*Dropping Names*
MAURA MOYNIHAN	*Masterji and Other Stories*
MUSHIRUL HASAN	*India Partitioned.* 2 vols
NAMITA GOKHALE	*Mountain Echoes*
NINA EPTON	*Mumtaz Mahal: Beloved Empress*
P. LAL	*The Bhagavad Gita*
RALPH RUSSELL	*The Famous Ghalib*
ROMESH BHANDARI	*Goa*
RUSKIN BOND	*Ruskin Bond's Green Book*
SHOVANA NARAYAN	*Rhythmic Echoes and Reflections: Kathak*
SUDHIR KAKAR (ed.)	*Indian Love Stories*
V.S. NARAVANE (ed.)	*Devdas and Other Stories by Sarat Chandra*

FORTHCOMING TITLES

SUMATI MUTATKAR	*Shrikrishna Narayan Ratanjankar –*
	A Many-Splendoured Genius
DHANALAKSHMI FORDYCE	*Purna Ghata*
MAJ. GEN. I. CARDOZO	*The Paramvir Chakra Winners*
SUJATA SABNIS	*A Twist in Destiny*

The
Story
of Tea

E. Jaiwant Paul

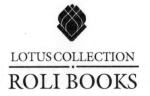

LOTUS COLLECTION
ROLI BOOKS

Dedicated
to
Shubh

Lotus Collection

© E. Jaiwant Paul 2001
All rights reserved. No part of this publication may
be reproduced or transmitted, in any form or by any
means, without the prior permission of the publisher.

This edition first published 2001
An imprint of
Roli Books Pvt Ltd
M-75, G.K. II Market
New Delhi 110 048
Phones: 6442271, 6462782, 6460886
Fax: 6467185
E-mail: roli@vsnl.com, Website: rolibooks.com
Also at
Varanasi, Agra, Jaipur and the Netherlands

ISBN: 81-7436-130-8
Rs. 225

Typeset in Galliard by Roli Books Pvt Ltd and
printed at Pauls Press, Okhla, New Delhi-110 020

Contents

Women pluckers are preferred because of their nimble fingers and dexterity.
They toil at least 8-10 hours, harvesting nearly 50,000 stems a day
in a typical Indian tea garden.

1

The Origin of Tea

*L*egend has it that tea originated in China in the dim reaches of history almost 5,000 years ago. This goes back to the time when the Pharaoh ruled in Egypt and the great settlements of Mohenjodaro and Harappa were established in north India, there were stirrings of civilisation in Babylon and Assyria and in Europe people lived in caves.

Emperor Shen Nung, who ruled China in the 28th century BC, was a legendary figure. He was known as the Divine Husbander and the credit for the plough, the hoe and the care of farm animals goes to him. He was not only a philosopher, but also interested in herbal medicine.

In an enchanting legend, once Shen Nung was sitting contemplatively in his garden. He was sipping a bowl of hot water when a gust of breeze blew a few leaves from a nearby tea plant, which grew wild in China, into the imperial bowl. The Emperor sniffed the fragrant brew, nodded his royal head with pleasure at this new aroma and drank it. As a beneficent ruler, he decided that such a wondrous brew should be shared with his subjects and thus tea was born. The date of this discovery is believed to be 2737 BC.

There is another story associated with the origin of tea, but set several centuries later and tied to the spread of Buddhism. It is believed that tea was introduced into China by Dharma, a grey-eyed monk from India who went to China in about AD 526 to spread the message of Buddhism. For many years the saint prayed and meditated without sleep. It so happened that during his sojourns, he was meditating in a temple at Honan province. But unfortunately, he grew drowsy and inadvertently fell asleep. He was so disgusted with this that he punished himself by cutting off his eyelids. He also discovered, by accident, that if he chewed the leaves of a particular shrub, he could remain alert. And this turned out to be the tea shrub. This enabled him to continue his meditations for several years more without sleep. Another improbable version of this story is that having cut off his eyelids, Dharma threw them and on the place where they fell sprang a tea shrub!

Moving on from legend to fact, it can be stated that the earliest mention of tea which modern scholars give credence to is found in the *Erh Ya* – an ancient Chinese dictionary published around 350 BC.

Tea was at first considered a medicinal herb and was infused from green untreated leaves. This must have tasted foul enough for most people to believe that it was doing them a great deal of good. Later, the Chinese found that a far better drink was possible if the leaves were allowed to wither and then dried by exposure to controlled heat before being infused. Once this was done tea was set on the path to popularity.

Beginning from the 8th century, tea became integral to the lives of the privileged classes in both China and Japan. It had become so popular that as is the way with governments, they thought it fit to levy a tax on tea.

The renowned author, Lu Yu, wrote his scholarly *Ch'a Ching*, a remarkable paean to tea, at the time of the Tang Dynasty (AD 618-907) when China had become the greatest empire in the world. By then tea had become more than just a drink, it was a symbol of hospitality and a ceremony. Lu Yu discoursed on the planting and manufacture of tea, the type of water to be used, the 24 different items of equipment and the method of preparing a cup of tea.

Lu Yu whimsically wrote, 'There are a thousand different appearances of tea leaves. Some leaves look like the Tartar's boots (wrinkled), some like the buffalo's breast (regular shaped), some look like the floating clouds arising from the mountains (curled), some like the ripples on the water caused by a breeze, some leaves look dull brown and some like a piece of newly cultivated land covered with puddles after a violent rain (uneven). These are good teas.' Yu Lu's poetic similes above suggest that tea leaves can be wrinkled or regular shaped, curled or uneven; descriptions which are not very different from those that the modern tea taster employs. Lu Yu became a sort of a patron saint for tea lovers. He summed up his philosophy in the now famous line of poetry, 'I am in no way interested in immortality, but only in the taste of tea.'

It is interesting to note that much of the advice contained in *Ch'a Ching* and the etiquette suggested are still followed to this day. Lu Yu further wrote, 'For exquisite freshness and vibrant fragrance, limit the number of cups to three. If one can be satisfied with less than perfection, five are permissible.'

Another Chinese poet was, however, more liberal about the quantity of tea to be drunk. He wrote, 'The first bowl soothes the throat, while the second banishes loneliness. At the third bowl, I search my soul and find 5,000 volumes of ancient poems. With the fourth bowl, a slight perspiration washes away all unhappy things. At the fifth bowl, my bones and muscles are cleansed. With the sixth bowl, I am in communication with the immortal spirit. The seventh bowl? It is forbidden: already a cool ethereal breeze begins to soothe my whole body.' It seems as if the second author was addicted to a beverage more potent than tea!

Lu Yu was also one of the earliest and most discerning tea tasters. 'Those who attribute smoothness, darkness and flatness to good tea are connoisseurs of an inferior order; those who attribute wrinkles, yellowness and uneven surface to good tea' (presumably tea leaves) 'are the ordinary connoisseurs; those who hold the opinion that these qualities may or may not belong to good tea are the superior connoisseurs because whether tea is good or otherwise depends upon its flavour.'

The renowned author goes on to say, 'Sometimes onion, ginger, jujube, orange peel and peppermint are boiled along with the tea. Alas! this is the slop water of a ditch.' He also had views on the beneficial aspects of tea. 'Boiled water is to quench thirst, wine to drown sorrow and tea to avoid sleepiness . . . when feeling hot and thirsty, suffering from headache, fatigue or pain in the joints one should drink tea.'

Tea the 'wondrous bud' was originally called *te*, but somehow down the ages the Chinese character for *te* was changed to *cha*, which is now the current term for tea. However, in certain Chinese dialects the word *te* was retained. Thus in Europe and America this is how the drink was popularly known. In India it is *cha* or *chai* and in Russia and Portugal it is a derivative of *cha*, while in Arabic it became *shai*.

By the 6th or 7th century although tea was available in the powdered form, the more popular form was brick tea. The leaves were harvested and powdered to enhance the aroma and flavour, and then they were, finally, pressed into moulds, which were heated over charcoal. These processes resulted in the production of brick tea. These bricks could be easily transported to all parts of the country. The processing of tea was, gradually, improved to produce more subtle and finer teas. However, brick tea remained popular till the 19th century and found a ready market not only in China, but also in Russia mainly because it was easier to transport.

Tea in China, gradually, became a mark of friendship and hospitality. It established a warm camaraderie and was served on all social occasions. The art of tea making reached its height from the 10th century onward under the Sung Dynasty, also famous for its pottery. Emperor Hui Tsun (1100-1126) was a connoisseur and wrote a treatise on tea. The Emperor's own serenity required a particularly pure form of tea. The imperial plucking method was used only for his tea. The leaves were plucked by young virgins wearing gloves. With the help of gold scissors they chopped only the bud and the youngest leaf. The leaves were then left on a golden platter to dry before being poured directly into the Emperor's bowl. Not everyone could aspire to such a degree of purity, and people generally gathered in tea houses known for their warmth, their floral decorations and calligraphed scrolls. There were also working-class tea houses that the famous traveller, Marco Polo felt 'were of dubious propriety, since somewhat bawdy ladies enlivened the atmosphere with songs'.

Tea crossed the seas and was introduced by the Chinese to their cousins in Japan as early as the 8th century. In AD 729, the Japanese Emperor presented China tea to one hundred priests, who attended a course on Zen Buddhism at the royal palace. Zen Buddhism developed as a reaction against the elaborate ritual and ceremony of organised Buddhism. When these priests returned, many of them planted the shrub in their own parishes. With this beginning it is understandable that tea became involved with religion. Zen monks, who drank tea to keep awake during long sessions of meditation, practised ritual tea drinking. It later became an actual part of Zen ritual, honouring the first patriarch from India, Dharma. However, tea gradually became a widely popular drink not just in temples, but in social gatherings throughout Japan. The tea house became an important institution and a special architecture called *chaseki* was developed for such a house. The concept was one of extreme simplicity of construction enhanced by a single decoration, which could be some calligraphy, painting or a flower arrangement. The tea house became the place for friends to gather, drink tea, and discuss the merits of different forms of art.

In the 9th century the success of tea led to the tea ceremony or *cha-no-yu* or *chado* meaning the way of tea. This time-honoured institution is still conducted in modern Japan. It is rooted in the principle of Zen Buddhism and based on the adoration of the beautiful amidst the sordid facts of everyday existence. It is an aesthetic way of entertaining guests, in which everything is done to an established order.

The most famous exponent of the tea ceremony was Sen Rikyu, an aesthete at the 16th century Japanese court. He codified the ceremony into a style known as *wabi* meaning simplicity, quietude and absence of ornament.

The historian, Lafcardio Hearn, writing in the last century has given a sensitive description of the tea ceremony. He says, 'It requires years of training and practice to graduate to the art . . . yet the whole of this art as to details signifies no more than the making and serving of a cup of tea. However, it is a real art – a most exquisite art. The actual making of the infusion is a matter of no consequence in itself: the supremely important matter is that the art be performed in the most perfect, most polite, most graceful, and most charming manner possible. Everything done from the kindling of the charcoal fire to the presentation of the tea – must be done according to rules of supreme etiquette. Rules requiring natural grace as well as great patience to fully master.' In this 1,000-year-old ceremony while the ritual is elaborate, its basic idea is simplicity and restraint.

I had the good fortune of attending a tea ceremony in Tokyo. Such ceremonies are usually performed in a separate area of the house known as *sukiya* or the Abode of Fancy. Guests have to cross a garden by a path of paved stones, the *roji* (earth damp with dew). They walk in silence, while the plants, moss and the singing of birds instil a mood of contemplation. Establishing harmony with nature is essential before the ceremony and this extends to the waiting room where flowers are arranged in a bamboo vase. After the guests have performed the purification ritual of rinsing their mouths and washing their hands in a small stone basin, they are seated in a central room decorated by a hanging scroll or painting selected according to the season or theme of the gathering.

The host serves a light Japanese meal, *kaiseki*, to each of the guests seated cross-legged on mats. Each dish, which comes from either the sea or the mountains, is savoured in three ways, 'with the eyes, the tongue and the heart'. Freshly cut chopsticks of green bamboo enhance the taste. After the meal is over, the guests go to the garden for some fresh air, and then they sit down once again to drink the strong tea.

This tea is prepared by heating the water in a kettle placed on a charcoal stove sunk into the middle of the floor. The water is poured into the teapot which contains the *matcha* or froth of liquid jade – a powdered green tea that is not steeped but whipped in the bowl with a small bamboo whisk. The host handles the teapot and according to tradition, the guests share the same bowl, each awaiting his or her turn. The host, who does not partake, patiently repeats the preparation never forgetting to greet the person who extends his hands for the bowl. Guests must hold the bowl in both hands, with the porcelain pattern turned towards the host. The tea is drunk three times in this manner.

After the tea-drinking ceremony is over, all the items used are then washed and put away. The host then offers a piece of cake to each guest followed by weaker tea served in a different bowl. The tea ceremony concludes in silent contemplation of the fire and the surroundings. The host then sees off his guests at the threshold and many an elegant bow is exchanged. An uninitiated observer may feel that nothing extraordinary has happened, but most experience a soothing tranquility of mind.

Sen Rikyu, the great exponent of the tea ceremony, was accused of treason towards his patron and was condemned to death. However, he was granted the honour of dying by his own hand. On the day destined for his self-immolation, He invited his chief disciples to the last tea ceremony. After the ceremony was over, the mournful guests bid their last farewell and left. Sen Rikyu wore his white death robe, gazed tenderly at the blade of the fatal sword and thus addressed it:

'Welcome to thee, O sword of eternity
Through Buddha and Dharma alike
Thou have cleft thy way.'

Then with a smile on his face, Sen Rikyu plunged the sword into his body and passed into the unknown.

The famous tea houses of Japan described earlier had their moment of glory in the 17th century. They were true pleasure houses where people sang songs, played music, and enjoyed themselves. In· recent decades they have been less popular due to the unfortunate Americanisation of Japan which has led to a drop in the consumption of tea in favour of other less civilised beverages. Japanese green tea is drunk in the morning to get a good start to the day, or before a meal to help digestion. The latest craze in Japan seems to be for scented blends and flavoured tea. True tea lovers hope that the Japanese youth will gradually rediscover the way of tea. For tea remains deeply etched in Japanese culture.

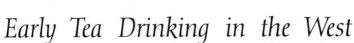

2

Early Tea Drinking in the West

*t*ill a few decades ago Britain was the greatest tea drinking country in the world. In recent years, however, it has been replaced by India, which started drinking more tea in sheer quantity than any other nation. This does not, obviously, apply in per capita terms but total quantity. In per capita terms, interestingly, no one can beat the Irish who down it by the gallon. Other important tea drinking nations are Russia, USA, Pakistan, Turkey, Iran, Iraq, Sudan, Egypt, Germany, Canada and Australia.

Tea is consumed by about one-half of the world's population which can be easily understood when one considers its popularity in two of the world's most populous nations – China and India. Despite this, however, it is second to coffee in commercial importance, largely because a significant portion of the world's tea crop is consumed in the growing regions and to that extent tea does not enter international transactions.

Whatever the statistics, Britain became the crucial and most enduring market for this commodity. For the British the hot cuppa is much more than a drink. An Englishman, Cecil Porter, wrote in a memorable paragraph, 'Tea is a solace, a mystique, an art, a way of life, almost a religion. It is more deeply traditional than the roast beef of old England. It is at least as characteristic of Britain as Yorkshire pudding, bowler-hats, rolled umbrellas, the Guards and fish and chips. This khaki-coloured concoction brewed, through an accident of history, from an exotic plant grown thousands of miles from fog, cricket and left-hand driving, has become the life blood of the nation.' Tea was a basic necessity for British soldiers in the two world wars of the last century. It was made crudely in buckets and served in large mugs holding almost a pint. The officers, of course, took their tea in fine cups and saucers. It is said that Britain could not have fought either of the two world wars without tea. Probably nowhere else in the world has a beverage so pleasantly governed the day of an entire nation. It is best symbolised by the early morning cuppa sipped on awakening.

G. Brochard in *The Book of Tea* recounts the story of a gentleman who was a guest of Baron Rothschild. 'Early in the morning, a liveried servant entered my room pushing a huge table on wheels. He asked, "Would you like tea or a peach, sir?" I chose tea, which immediately provoked another question, "China, India or Ceylon, sir?" When I asked for India tea he enquired, "With lemon, cream or milk, sir?" I opted for milk, but he wanted to know which breed of cow I preferred, "Jersey, Hereford or Sorthorn, sir?" Never had I drunk such a good cup of tea.'

Despite this Britain was late on the tea scene, after several other European nations. By the 8th century, tea had become an essential part of the pattern of life, culture and religion in China and Japan. It was several centuries before Europe was even aware of this commodity. This is very surprising because tea had started going westward along with other exotic goods from China around the 7th and 8th centuries by the caravans from Persia. Other than Persia, tea was being drunk in the palaces of Samarkand and Bukhara. In the 12th and 13th centuries, the European crusaders had arrived on the west Asian shores of the Mediterranean and they handled a considerable amount of trade from the East, strangely, without discovering tea.

In Europe, tea was first mentioned in literature in 1559 as *chai catai* (tea from China) in *Navigational Viaggi* (Voyages and Travels) by Gain Battista Romusio, a noted Venetian author. Venice was then the gateway for the trade between Asia and Europe. Romusio wrote that he had heard from a Persian traveller about this herb and that people in Szechwan were accustomed to infuse it in boiling water and it aided stomach-aches and gout. Thereafter, several sailors, missionaries and merchants brought back stories of the tea plant and of the drink which was not only a medicine but was valued also 'on account of a peculiar mild bitterness, not disagreeable to the taste' – a rather apt description!

The Portuguese were the first Europeans to establish a trading centre at Macau on the Chinese coast in 1557. They were also the first to set foot in Japan. Several Portuguese Jesuit priests wrote home about the amazing medicinal qualities of tea. However, the influence of Portugal in the East declined and that of Holland took

its place. It was the Dutch who first brought tea to
Europe and the first consignment is believed to have
reached Holland in 1610 along with spices, silks and
other luxuries. The Dutch in, due course, opened up tea
plantations in Java and by 1640 were shipping home
large quantities. Initially, tea here had become a popular
drink only amongst the aristocrats and wealthy merchants,
but later it spread among the common people as well.
D. Maitland in his book, *5,000 Years of Tea* says, 'Before
tea was shipped in enough volume to sell at a reasonable
price, outlandish tea gatherings were held that resembled
bizarre parodies of the Japanese tea ceremony. Tea that
cost the equivalent of $100 per pound was served from
silver and porcelain containers with much pomp and
ceremony. Sugar and saffron were added to the beverage,
which was sipped noisily from saucers. Conversations were
monopolised by tea and the rich cakes served with it.
When as many as fifty cups had been drunk by each
guest, brandy, sugar, raisins and pipes – smoked by the
women as well as the men – ended the party.' It almost
sounds like a tea orgy – 50 cups!

W.H. Ukers in his long and remarkable book: *All
About Tea* mentions a Dutch writer, Linschoten, who
served as an official in Goa for several years in the 1580s.
His book was translated into English and his interesting
account of tea drinking in Japan deserves quotation:
'Every man hath a table alone, without tablecloths or
napkins, and eateth with two pieces of wood like the
men of China; they drink wine of Rice, wherewith they
drink themselves drunk and after their meat use a certain
drink, which is a pot with hot water, which they drink
as hot as ever they may endure, whether it be winter or
summer . . . the aftersaid warm water is made with

powder of a certain hearbe call *chaa*, which is much esteemed . . . when they entertain any of their friends, they give them some of that warm water to drink; for the pots where they sieth it and wherein the hearbe is kept, with the earthen cups which they drink it in, they esteem as much of them as we do of Diamonds, Rubies and other precious stones and they are not esteemed for their newness but for their oldness and for that they were made by good workmen.'

L. Wickham, agent of the East India Company on the Japanese island of Hirado, is credited with being the first Englishman to have mentioned tea in writing. There is a letter in the India Office Records dated June 27, 1615, which Wickham sent to a colleague at Macau asking him to send a pot of 'the best sort of *chaw*'. There is no definite evidence as to the date when tea was introduced in England. The first public sale of tea in England was, however, conducted by Thomas Garraway in 1657. It is surmised that the first supplies were from Holland.

This sale was of historic importance. For this, Thomas Garraway published and distributed a poster. It is a bizarre example of quackery and hard sell and will make today's promoters of pharmaceuticals writhe with envy.

> The leaf is of such known virtues that those very nations famous for Antiquity, Knowledge and Wisdom do frequently sell it among themselves for twice its weight in silver . . .
> It maketh the body active and lusty.
> It helpeth the Headache, Giddiness and Heaviness thereof.

*It is very good against stone and Gravel,
cleaning the Kidneys and Ureter.*

*It is good against Crudities, strengthening
the weakness of the Ventricle or Stomack,
causing good Appetite and Digestion and
particularly for Men of a corpulent body
and such as are great eaters of flesh.*

*It vanquisheth heavy dreams, easeth the
Brain and strengtheneth the Memory.*

*It prevents and cures ague, surfeits . . .
and fevers, by infusing a fit quantity of the
Leaf, thereby provoking a most gentle vomit . . .*

*It being prepared and drunk with Milk
and Water strengtheneth the inward parts
and prevents consumptions and powerfully
asswageth the pains of the Bowels or griping
of the guts and looseness.*

*It drives away all pains in the Collick
proceeding from Wind and purgeth safely the
Gall . . .*

And many believed what Thomas Garraway said.

Interestingly coffee had arrived in England about a
few years earlier. From its original home in Ethiopia, it
had spread to Arabia and reached Constantinople and
Cairo and then Venice. A merchant from Turkey had
brought coffee to London and it gained quick popularity
as a beverage in the London coffee houses, the first of
which was established by a Greek in 1652. The coffee
houses flourished in London and many other cities and
became centres of political, social, literary and business
influence where many a deal was clinched. Coffee houses

did not restrict themselves to the sale of coffee, but supplied alcoholic drinks as well. Soon it was found that a place could be found for tea on the menu.

The *Gazette* of September 9, 1658, announced the news of the death of the Lord Protector, Oliver Cromwell. But its columns also carried an advertisement of historic interest inserted by the proprietor of the Sultaness Coffee House.

> That excellent and by all physicians approved China drink called by the Chinaans *teha*, by other nations *tay* alias tea is sold at the Sultaness Head Copphee House in Sweetings Rents, by the Royal Exchange, London.

This announcement was preceded by an advertisement offering a reward for the apprehension of a horse thief!

This is reported to be the first advertisement for any commodity in a London newspaper and may be considered a landmark not only in the history of tea, but also in the history of advertising.

Garraway's preposterous advertising was probably taken seriously, for tea, gradually, became popular as more people tried the new drink. As in Holland, it was the aristocrats who were the first enthusiasts for the new brew. This is understandable because tea at the time was very expensive. Garraway's prices ranged between 16 to 60 shillings per pound.

King Charles II married the Portuguese princess Catherine of Braganza in 1662, and part of the dowry was the island of Bombay, which King Charles promptly leased to the East India Company for the princely sum of £10 per year. Catherine was an inveterate tea drinker and the habit was soon established in British court circles. After the East India Company opened up a trading post in the

East, the Directors presented Charles II with a gift of tea. Apparently the king kept exotic birds and animals and as Deny Forrest says in *Tea for the British*, 'The story is a quaint one. The East India Company was under continual pressure to augment the collection. So when a fleet returned from Java on July 12, 1664, the Court of Directors ordered Captain Prowde to go on board the ships and enquire what rarities of birds, beasts and other curiosities had been brought back this time. Alas, it had to be reported that the factors having failed in every place to send home anything suitable as a present for the King, the Company's officials had taken a rather despairing look around and decided that His Majesty would have to make do with some miscellaneous goodies, including a silver case of oil of cinnamon and some good tea.' The gift of tea must have been a success with the king as 18 months later a larger quantity was offered – 22 pounds!

In 1660 the famous diarist, Samuel Pepys, wrote, 'Did send for a cup of tea, a China drink, which I had never drunk before.' Apparently he enjoyed it, for a few years later there is another entry in his diary, 'Home, and there I find my wife making tea, which Mr Pelling, the potticary, tells her is good for her cold and defluxions.'

Dr Samuel Johnson the lexicographer, who created his huge English dictionary single-handed must have done so under the stimulation of tea as he was passionately fond of it and describes himself as 'a hardened and shameless tea drinker, whose kettle has scarcely time to cool, who with tea amuses the evening, with tea solaces the midnight and with tea welcomes the morning'. His teapot held ten cups. At the house of a distinguished lady, he kept passing his cup for more, until he had drunk 32 cups. The lady said, 'Dr Johnson, you drink

too much tea.' Johnson said, 'Madam, you are insolent.'
However, since tea was expensive and not particularly
nutritious, Johnson maintained that 'it was a liquor not
proper for the lower classes of the people'.

Despite Johnson's view, the popularity of tea also grew
among the lower classes. However, lack of familiarity
with the brew led to many a droll situation. Schafer in
Teacraft says, 'Tea was sometimes mysterious, dear and
quite puzzling. Some took tea with salt, ginger and
nutmeg. A Jesuit who enjoyed tea in China added eggs
to his tea. Schoolboys spread used leaves on their bread.
A country housewife thrilled with her first pound of the
fashionable stuff, invited neighbours to share it. She
boiled and served it rather like spinach with salt and
butter. Her guests detested it.' Another expert advocated
smoking tea like tobacco, after having lightly dampened
the leaves with a sprinkling of brandy and went on to
add that the sediment or ashes remaining in the bowl of
the pipe was marvellous for whitening the teeth.

As tea drinking became general, a British
commentator made a complaint in 1767, which is a
familiar one even today. He said, 'Labourers are losing
their time to come and go to the tea table; nay farmer's
servants are even demanding tea for breakfast with the
maids.' He went on to say that 'as much superfluous
money is wasted on tea and sugar as would maintain
four million more subjects on bread'.

As tea was now coming into the country in increasing
quantities, the British Government thought it was
a splendid source of revenue and a tax of eight pence
a gallon was imposed on tea, oddly enough, in its
liquid form or infusion. Under this system the tea had
to be made in bulk to await the taxman or gauger

and reheated once or twice a day before sale to the customer.

Tea was sold in 2,000 or so coffee houses in London and the procedure of taxing tea in its liquid form was both cumbersome and expensive. In addition, it must have been disastrous for the flavour. After about 20 years of this absurd system of taxation, the government thought of a more sensible way of taxing tea and a duty of 5 shillings per pound was imposed on the dry leaf. As the tea trade was an East India Company monopoly, tax could be collected from the warehouses of the company in London before release into the market. This tax was a huge sum in those days, and as the price of tea went up the inevitable result was the smuggling of tea. The decline of the coffee houses had led to the popularity of tea, and by the middle of the 18th century, tea had established its position as the national drink. The tax, meanwhile, kept on increasing and in 1773 it represented 64 per cent of the value of tea. It was soon getting out of reach for the common people and there was much wringing of hands. Smuggling of tea became highly profitable and developed into a considerable industry. It was also the only way of providing cheaper tea. It is estimated that more than half the tea consumed in Britain at that time was contraband and according to some calculation the smuggler had two-thirds of it. Ships from Holland, Portugal and various other European countries were carrying tea for eventual smuggling into the United Kingdom. Smuggling became so rampant that members of the Board of Trade were 'wallowing in contraband wine, tea and silk. The caves of England were full of untaxed luxuries and so were the crypts of country churches'. The latter, it is reported, with the connivance of the vicar!

Often the officials of the East India Company and His Majesty's Customs and Excise looked the other way if the bribe was high enough. Smugglers even met Company ships returning from China at the entrance of the English Channel and bought tea from their captains. Consumers, however, found that even smuggled tea was expensive and, therefore, adulteration became widespread, as this was another way to make tea cheaper. It was adulterated with sloe leaves, used tea leaves, liquorice, ash tree leaves and various other offensive materials including, it is reported, specially treated sheep's dung.

Ultimately the smuggling and adulteration became so rampant that in 1784, William Pitt, the Prime Minister, slashed the import duty to 12½ per cent, and smuggling disappeared as there was no longer any profit in it. According to some commentators, obviously biased, this was the most useful thing Pitt ever did.

Either because tea was expensive or from the fashion in China, it was drunk very weak. Sugar must have always been popular. The innovation of taking milk with tea is credited to the French, specifically to Madame de Servigne. Milk was going through one of its phases of being in favour with doctors, and it was a fashionable cure for everything. The flavour of China tea is at all times extremely delicate and the addition of milk is best with stronger tea. Some of the paintings of families at tea or of tea tables, show that while in the late 1600s there were sugar bowls and the tea kettle itself, the milk jug was missing. Interestingly, several paintings show handleless china cups. In the later paintings, little silver jugs for milk, matching the teapot, started making an appearance.

With the reduction in duty, the tea became cheaper,

and the British consumer could afford to buy more of it. Consequently its popularity grew. It was brewed in every native home from the hovel to the manor. Millions of people had started drinking tea in the afternoon without inventing the ritual of afternoon tea. The credit for this innovation has been given to the Duchess of Bedford, probably because she was a Duchess!

In almost all the literature on tea, the seventh Duke of Bedford and his Duchess Anna are mentioned as the early promoters of tea. D. Maitland says, 'In the 1790s, the Duke imported 10 pounds of tea as well as utensils for drinking tea and may well have been the first to launch a new term into the household vocabulary in England – China teaset. His wife, on the other hand, is credited with pioneering the essential ritual that ultimately doomed Britain to wholesale addiction – the ritual of taking tea.

'Up until that time, meal times in England were a lusty almost barbaric affair of red meat and ale. Country houses in their day provided prodigious breakfasts with joints of meat on the sideboard. Sportsmen drank ale scorning such slops as tea. And they went hungry until dinner time about 8 p.m. Lunch as a meal did not exist. The Duchess of Bedford to put a stop to this punishing routine introduced tea at 5 p.m. in her room . . . she served it with cakes . . . By degrees, afternoon tea became the fashion.'

The East India Company tea imported into England was partly bought from Chinese traders in Java and partly from Portuguese traders in Surat (India). In 1685, the Chinese Emperor opened his ports to European traders. England took immediate advantage of this concession, and by 1700 it had established a firm base at Canton. In

1721, the East India Company was granted a monopoly of tea imports into England. Consumption rose from 20,000 pounds in 1700 to a million pounds in 1785. The East India Company was thus handling vast quantities of tea and these were disposed off by auction four times a year. A limited number of brokers used to bid at the auctions for their wholesale and retail clients. Tea was sold 'by the candle'. A candle was lit and the auction of one lot of tea would start with bids coming from various buyers. As soon as an inch of the candle burnt away, the highest bid was accepted and the hammer fell. Then the next lot was auctioned. Later the amount of tea required in England increased and the quarterly auctions became increasingly longer until they occupied many days of frenzied and furious business. Strangely, no one thought to increase the number of auctions to more than four a year.

About the middle of the 18th century, there was a bizarre controversy about tea. Tea had been beatified by the poet William Cowper as 'the cups that cheer but not inebriate'. But others had reviled it, strangely, on medical grounds. The attack was led by John Wesley, founder of the Methodist Church, who wrote, 'Having an exceedingly good constitution and being otherwise in health, I was surprised at some symptoms of a paralytic disorder,' which he attributed to drinking tea. He found that it had the same effect on his friends who drank tea and that their 'nerves were all unstrung and bodily strength all decayed'. Wesley decided to give up tea and he said that for three days his head ached and he remained half asleep. At the end of this period, his memory had completely failed, and then he had to resort to prayer, remain on his knees for hours and was finally, a 'cured man'. Sounds somewhat like the withdrawal symptoms suffered by a present day drug addict!

Another fanatical propagandist against tea was Jonas Hanway. He equated tea with gin in its power to harm and felt it was destroying the nation. He also had the harebrained notion that tea was a destroyer of female beauty and dolefully wrote to a lady of his acquaintance in a series of letters. 'Your very chambermaids have lost their bloom by sipping tea . . . and how many thousands,' he asks, 'are annually poisoned by tea, gin and wine?'

Even Samuel Johnson joined the fray against tea. Johnson's argument was, however, more economic as he said, 'If tea is thus pernicious, if it impoverishes our country, if it raises temptation and gives opportunity to illicit commerce (smuggling) . . . let us at once resolve to prohibit if for ever.' Despite his convictions Johnson continued to relish his tea and 'was impatient to be served and swallowed it down in haste'.

Deny Forrest has quoted the argument of a politician and journalist, who offers to prove tea's corrosive, gnawing, poisonous power, by putting 'it to the test with a lean hog. Give him fifteen bushels of malt and he will repay you with ten scores of bacon. But give him 730 tea messes, and nothing else, and at the end of about seven days he is dead with hunger'.

Dr Thomas Short published his *Discourse on Tea* about this time. He wrote, 'This leaf, like all other things has met with various treatment, according to the different Tastes, Humours and prejudices of mankind. Some have ascribed to it such sovereign healing Virtues, as though it were not only capable to extirpate and prevent the cause of all diseases, but even almost to raise up and restore those that have come to their last agonising moments. Others are no less severe in their censures and declamations . . . accounting it no better than a slow, but efficacious poison.' Dr Short, however, went on to show that he was a strong champion of tea and from clinical experience recommended tea as a remedy for many types of ailments as had Garraway's advertisement.

Fortunately, the whole controversy proved to be an irrelevance and the consumption increased till it could be described as a national addiction. Hanway, Wesley, Johnson and others failed to see that tea drinking among the lower classes helped to combat their heavy consumption of alcohol. This was at a time when gin shops invited customers 'to come inside and get drunk for a penny and dead drunk for two pence'. In fact, tea was recognised as the most effective weapon in the armour of temperance reformers and it has been suggested that there is a connection between the words 'tea' and 'teetotal'.

Tea so far had a fairly humble and lowly place in the story of mankind, but then suddenly it seemed to assume a huge and exaggerated role, so much so, that it altered or rather speeded up the very course of world history. We are referring, of course, to the Boston Tea Party. Tea had by now established itself very firmly on the east coast of North America. It had been first introduced by the Dutch around 1650, and had become fashionable in New Amsterdam. When the English captured the town from the Dutch they renamed it New York. Tea continued to prosper not only here, but also all over the Atlantic seaboard. By the 1760s, the American colonies were importing about one million pounds of tea annually. It was the third largest colonial import at the time behind textiles and manufactured goods. The British companies supplied most of this tea, and the price carried a huge element of tax. Consequently, three-quarters of the tea was smuggled into America. In 1764, the Stamp Act was passed by the British Parliament asserting the right to impose tax on colonists. This caused protests and there was a boycott of British goods. British tea exports to America dropped drastically. Two years later the Stamp Act was repealed, but it was later replaced by the Tea Act which retained the intolerable duty of 3 pence per pound. Indignation in America ran high and there were many demonstrations in Boston. People were exhorted to give up tea and many patriots did that and resorted to substitutes. Tea became that 'worst of plagues, detested tea'. This fiddling with taxation on tea had epoch-making consequences, and was a tremendous blunder for Britain, hastening the loss of the American colonies.

About this time the East India Company ran into a financial crisis as it owed the government one million pounds sterling, which it was unable to repay. This coincided with a surplus of tea stocks in England which the Company could not liquidate either. The East India Company was, therefore, permitted to sell the export surplus to America with the hated tax of 3 pence per pound. The ships carrying the tea arrived off Boston in November and December 1773. Tempers ran high, furious public protests were made and messages were passed about 'mingling tea with salt water'. A band of 50 or 60 men boarded the British ships, broke open the tea chests with hatchets and clubs and threw the tea into the sea. 'Imaginative engravings show them elaborately disguised as Redskins but, in fact, most of them made do with a dab of paint or lamp black and an old blanket round the shoulders.' A total of 342 chests of tea valued at £10,000 were thrown into the sea, while the crowds lustily cheered. This Tea Party was repeated in several other places including New York, Philadelphia, Annapolis and Greenwich, where tea cargoes were destroyed or refused a landing. In each place the destruction of tea was followed by riots 'stunning the British Government with a new and startling method of diplomacy'.

The War of Independence was soon sparked off and in 1776, the Americans drew up the Declaration of Independence. Tea became a symbol of oppression and patriots refused to drink it. Ever since Americans drink far more coffee than tea.

Other than Britain another great tea-drinking nation was Russia. As early as 1618, the Chinese presented Czar Alexis with several chests of tea and while it met with immediate success at court, it took two hundred years for it to become a common drink in the land of vodka. Regular camel caravans began transporting vast quantities of tea via Mongolia following a very difficult and circuitous route. The entire journey from China to Russia was 11,000 miles, and took almost a year and a half. Tea was first shipped from the tea-growing areas to the northern part of Tientsin. It then had to be transported 200 miles over steep mountains by horses and mules to Kalgan, north-west of Peking. It was then transferred to camels and carried across the dreaded Gobi Desert to Kayakhta, and then on to Russia. The Trans-Siberian Railway was completed in 1905, after which tea only took seven weeks to reach Russia and the mighty caravans passed into oblivion. Russian Caravan Tea, which had a marked flavour of adventure and was spoken of with pride, was likewise forgotten.

Hot tea was the ideal beverage for the freezing climate of Russia. The typical samovar is a large urn of water with a broad tube going up the middle filled with red-hot coal, which ensures an unending supply of boiling water. The water is drawn off by means of a tap into an ordinary teapot containing tea leaves. The tea is made very strong and poured into a glass, filling it partially and then topping it off with more boiling water from the samovar. The tea is generally drunk with lemon. The Russians like their tea with sugar, but instead of mixing it with the tea, the peasants put a lump of sugar into their mouth and then drink the tea through the sugar. Another alternative is to put a spoon of jam into the tea instead of lemon and this is known as jam tea.

Tea lovers leave the samovar bubbling – 'or growling like a storm' – in their sitting room all day long. All great Russian authors, from Dostoevski to Tolstoy to Gorky and Pushkin have written about the warm intimacy created by a samovar. The former Soviet Union became a tea-producing country, and there are considerable tea estates in Georgia, but the domestic demand is still not met and the quality of tea is poor. Today Russia is an important buyer of Indian tea and takes a significant proportion of delicately flavoured Darjeeling teas and good Assams at attractive prices and will continue to do so in the future.

3

The China Tea Trade

*I*t is now necessary to take a look at the China-end of the tea trade. So far China was the only source of supply for the West, but it was a difficult country to deal with, as seems to be the case even today. China has been characterised by exclusiveness from the beginning, for the Chinese considered that their country and culture represented the apex of civilisation. China was the great Middle Kingdom of the Earth and all other countries were barbaric and inferior. Their Emperor was the son of Heaven; none could thus be his equal. The Chinese kept their country completely closed with no contact with outsiders. However, one of the Manchu Emperors, K'ang-hi (1662-1722), changed tack and eager for trade opened his ports. Wasting little time, many Portuguese and British traders entered the country but, unfortunately, their conduct over the next few years did not impress the Chinese favourably. To quote P.J. Banyard in *A History of Tea Trade*, 'Any distinctions they made between the barbarians was a droll and disparaging one. By their reckoning the Portuguese were distinguished by their ungovernable lust for women, the French by their liking for warfare and the British by their craving for money.'

In order to protect the people from the evil influences of the 'foreign devils' trade was then restricted to the single port of Canton and several other limitations were placed on their activities. All the Europeans were described as living in rat-infested ghettos. Their factories were huddled against each other, with the flag of each country flying in front. Not only were they denied all contact, but the Chinese were forbidden to teach their language to the barbarians under pain of death. Chinese proclamations and instructions to the Europeans ended with the closing command, 'Tremble fearfully hereat. Instantly obey.'

A group of Chinese merchants known as *co-hong* were the only people permitted to trade with the foreigners and be their contact with China. The only port through which the foreigners were allowed to trade was Canton. The *co-hong* always consisted of thirteen Chinese merchants and they got their name because their *hongs* or warehouses were near the factories of the foreigners. There were thirteen of these factories ranged along the waterfront, one for the French, one for the British, one for the Dutch, and so on. The *co-hong* were also made responsible for any misbehaviour on the part of · the barbarians and if they did act up, the *co-hong* merchants were punished and fined. As these Chinese merchants made excellent profits, they saw to it that the foreigners did not forget their place in the order of things. For over a century the system worked. The *co-hong* merchants had the reputation of being scrupulous in their financial dealings in the days when written documents were unknown.

The Europeans thus had no contact with the Chinese Government or other officials. Various British efforts at obtaining proper trading agreements with the Chinese were dismissed with contempt, and British envoys and delegations were treated at the Imperial Court as lackeys who had come to pay tribute. In 1795, a British delegation under Lord Macartney sought an audience with the Chinese Emperor, but to their great discomfiture they were denied the normal diplomatic courtesy and treated more as a bunch of barbarians who had come to pay tribute to his Imperial Majesty. The presents accepted, they were dismissed and sent packing. In 1816, another effort by Lord Amherst was also accorded the same rough treatment. Britain, by this time, had become the most important European trader with China, and accepted the indignities because of the enormous profits in the burgeoning tea trade.

The East India Company still had the monopoly for the China trade on tea and other luxuries, and they sought to retain this monopoly by exaggerating to the British Government the difficulty of dealing with the Chinese except on an exclusive company basis. Meanwhile, many competitors of the East India Company in Britain were struggling to break this monopoly. Their chief argument was that the Company kept the prices artificially high and thus inhibited the expansion of sales. But the British Government continued to favour the Company.

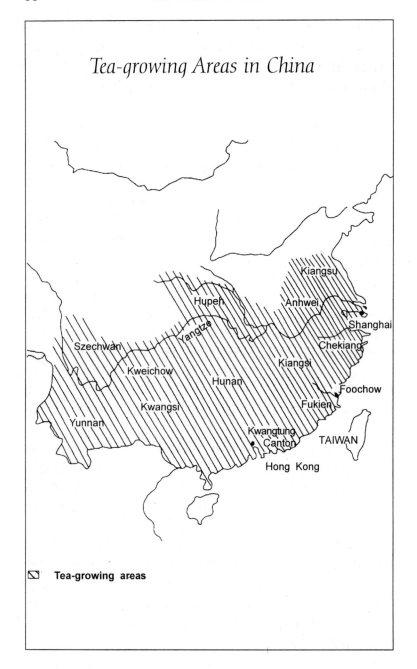

Tea-growing Areas in China

The trade with China was, however, one sided and constantly threatened Britain with a crippling deficit. While the demand for tea was enormous, the Chinese Government had no interest in anything that Britain had to offer in return. The only commodity they would accept was silver bullion. This could not carry on indefinitely without causing a significant decrease in Britain's treasury reserves. Britain, therefore, hit upon the dishonourable idea of narcotic traffic. The odious and addictive drug opium was banned in China. It was, however, cultivated in Bengal, which had by now fallen into British hands. To circumvent the trade imbalance the British started exporting it to China. This country was then associated with opium dens, addicts and crimes – a sorry image!

Since the opium trade was strictly prohibited in China, the East India Company decided not to risk its own valuable tea trade by openly hawking the drug. Instead it arranged auctions at Calcutta where opium was bought by independent British and Parsi traders, who then shipped it to Canton. Soon the Canton market seemed too small and restrictive and the opium traffickers sent ships upriver and along the South China coast in contravention of Chinese law and unloaded wherever they could find buyers. The opium trade was so enormous that it dwarfed all other Indian exports like cotton and spices. By the 1830s, opium sales contributed an astonishing one-fifth of all revenues of the British in those parts of India which had been occupied by them.

This trade, naturally, infuriated the Chinese Emperor and he sent a high official of irreproachable honesty, Lin Ze-Xu, to Canton with firm orders to curb the menace. He confiscated all opium in warehouses at Canton owned by British merchants and destroyed it. The British initially complied with the new orders, but they soon found an excuse to launch an attack with their vastly superior naval forces. The British and the French jointly fought the first opium war in 1848 and the second in 1856. The Chinese were forced to sign the Treaty of Tientsin, which resulted in the opening of China to European trade, but it did nothing to curb the opium trade. Many a British fortune was made by this murderous traffic.

As an aftermath of the war, the British took possession of an island, which at the time was described as 'a barren rock with hardly a house upon it'. It was called Hong Kong and this gave them a safe trading post.

The opium trade continued till 1908 as Hong Kong was enriched by spreading addiction and ruin within mainland China. The names of modern Hong Kong's biggest conglomerates are reminders of where the initial capital for these giant businesses came from. These conglomerates were among the largest drug peddlers the world has known, out selling today's Colombian mafia by miles. It is pointless to pretend that the drug trade then was different from its modern version. It was as deadly as it is today and was described and condemned then in exactly the same terms as it is now.

In 1834, after 113 years, the British Government had, finally, succumbed to the pressure of the free merchants and ended the monopoly of the East India Company. Very soon several merchant houses were scrambling to get a piece of this trade and were outdoing each other in the race to establish links with Canton.

During the long years of the East India Company's monopoly of the commerce with China, tea and other goods from there were carried in fleets of stately and

impressive ships known as East India Men. These heavy
ships were armed with cannons as in the early days of
trade, piracy was not uncommon. They used to haul
their cargoes at a leisurely pace halfway across the world
to Liverpool and London. The round trip would take 20
to 21 months. By the 1830s, the East India Men were
carrying 30 million pounds of tea.

The storage on these ships was organised in such a
way so as to keep the tea dry and fit for drinking after
the many months of a sweltering and clammy voyage,
while the smelly bilge slopped to and fro. This was done
by putting not tea but china in the lowest tier. Above
the china came the cheap grades of tea like Bohea. It
was only in the higher tiers that the fine grades like
Hysons and Gunpowders were stored, well above the
waterline. Above the teas, the highest storage was
reserved for silk and other luxury goods.

With the abolition of the Company's monopoly, the
free merchants began to look for faster vessels than the
slow and cumbersome East India Men. The Americans
had been developing a sailing ship with a daringly new
design. It was a three-masted, fully-rigged vessel with
fine lines and a great turn of speed. Thus was born the
Yankee clipper, which was ideally suited for the tea trade.
Speed was of the essence as the first plucked leaf of the
year was the prized 'First Chop' and premium prices
went to the first teas to reach the salesrooms in London's
Mincing Lane where the tea auctions took place.

The first American clipper, *The Oriental*, brought
1,600 tons of tea to London in 97 days as against the
21 months taken by East India Men. Her owners
demanded and were paid a freight fee that represented
three-quarters of the cost of constructing the ship. Soon

these clippers were ousting the slow British ships from their own home trade. British ship owners finally, awoke to the danger of this competition. Jardine, Matheson Company, a great China trading house, and others began building their own clippers and by 1853 had caught up with the Americans. A few years later, the American Civil War broke out and this further helped divert American competition elsewhere enabling British ships to get back on the scene.

Each year the clippers raced to be the first ship to reach English shores with tea. The first cargo would fetch a premium of as much as 6 pence a pound at the auction in Mincing Lane. And so began the Great Tea Races of the 1860s, an event that was second only to the Derby and heavy bets were laid on the result. The tea clippers would leave the Canton River on the same tide with a highly skilled crew of 30 men. They would race across the Indian Ocean, around the Cape of Good Hope, up the Atlantic and into the English Channel. The progress in the Channel would be watched with great public interest. The race would not finish until chests of tea were hurled for waiting clerks to draw samples and rush them to Mincing Lane. Generous cash rewards were given to the winning captains and crew.

The greatest race of all was that of 1866, which ended as a dead heat. Eleven ships left Foochow on the same tide and set course for England. They often covered over 300 miles a day and some of them remained in sight of each other. After rounding the Cape, the four ships – *Taeping*, *Ariel*, *Serica* and *Fiery Cross* – kept in the lead. From each headland news of their positions was telegraphed to the owners and excitement kept mounting in London. *Ariel* flew past through the water to enter the Channel just ten minutes ahead of the reputed *Taeping* followed a few hours later by *Serica*. In the end the result was declared a draw as all three berthed within hours of each other and on the same tide. A fantastically close finish considering that they had sailed half way round the world!

There is much romantic literature devoted to the great clipper races but looking at it factually, the era of clippers was brief and lasted a little over 20 years with the most avid and the fastest races taking place in the decade 1860-1870. The race of 1866, one of the most famous, was also one of the last. Steamships had been around for sometime but they could not compete because their cargo-carrying capacity was severely reduced by the amount of coal they had to take aboard for the long journey around the southern tip of Africa. But when the Suez Canal was opened in 1869 the steamships became an economic proposition for the first time and the beautiful clippers faded into history. Some steamers using the new route through the Suez Canal could do the passage in a matter of 44 days as against the 100 days or so taken by the faster clippers around the Cape of Good Hope. Only one of these famous tea clippers remains to be seen today, the *Cutty Sark*, which is a tourist attraction in dry dock at Greenwich in England.

At about this time a decisive development took place in the tea industry. China lost its monopoly in tea growing and started losing its market share in the tea trade. The new leaders emerging on the horizon were India and Sri Lanka. The basic explanation for the failure of China tea in the world markets of the first half of the 20th century is simply that the industry failed to move with the times. China tea was still grown by the peasants on their smallholdings and could not compete with the great plantations of India and Sri Lanka, where large amounts of capital were invested and where the climate allowed plucking to continue for the greater part of the year with higher financial returns. In addition, Indian and Sri Lankan teas were excellent in quality and easier to grade and classify.

By 1890, the tea production in India increased significantly and it replaced China as the leading tea exporter with Sri Lanka not far behind. From then on China tea went into a catastrophic decline. Of course, tea is still grown by the Chinese on an enormous scale for local consumption and some continues to be sent overland to Russia. But after 350 years, China tea ceased to be a player on the international scene.

4

Tea in India

the Europeans always believed that Chinese black tea such as Bohea and the green tea such as Singlo and Hyson came from different plants. It was only when they were exploring the possibility of growing tea in India that they realised that there is only one species of the tea plant, *Camellia sinensis*. They also came to know that the difference in black and green tea was the result of difference in cultivation and treatment. Black tea is first fermented and then fired or dried out by heat while green tea is unfermented.

It also took the British a long time to realise that *Camellia sinensis* was indigenous to India, and was growing wild in the districts running from Nepal eastward along the mountainous regions and forests of Assam to the Chinese provinces of Szechwan and Yunnan. Here the best Chinese tea was cultivated. What must have made identification of the tea plant more difficult was that in its wild untrammelled form the plant grew into a tree rising to a height of 30 feet, rather than the more familiar bush which was reduced by cultivation. The Assamese tribes had drunk tea for centuries and, indeed, in the north-eastern part of the Brahmaputra Valley in Assam, a number of tea bushes grew close together forming what were known as tea tracts. Tea had been planted and cultivated there by these tribes, particularly the Singhpos, from the distant past.

The proposal to cultivate tea in India goes back a long way. As early as 1778, Sir Joseph Banks, a well-known naturalist, drew up a scheme for its cultivation in India as it was 'an article of the greatest national importance to Britain'. He said that tea would do well between the 26th and 30th parallel of latitude and identified Bhutan and Cooch Behar (West Bengal) as suitable for large-scale cultivation.

In spite of Sir Joseph Banks' enthusiastic report on the cultivation of tea, nothing was done about it for 45 years, and it may be surmised that this was because the East India Company, having a monopoly of the China trade, took no interest in the possibility of growing it in India. In fact, they discouraged any such development. To understand this attitude, there are two factors to be considered. The first is that what are now the north Indian tea districts were not then British territory. Second, it took many more years before the indigenous Assam plant could be identified as tea by competent authorities.

The credit for this should go to Robert Bruce, who was an adventurer and a trader. He was aided in this by

Maniram Dutta Barua, an Assamese who was popularly known as Maniram Divan, who informed him of the existence of wild tea bushes. After seeing a picture of a tea plant, he is reported to have said, 'But we have it growing wild in our jungles.' He then guided Bruce to the abode of the Singhpo tribe, who had been cultivating it for ages. It was from them that Bruce obtained some specimens of the tea plant.

Robert was joined by his brother, C.A. Bruce, who was in service in charge of a flotilla of gunboats at Suddiya in Assam. C.A. Bruce planted some of the tea plants obtained from the Singhpos and sent the rest to Calcutta for identification. However, identification was not possible without seeds or flowers. The leaves, however, were pronounced to be of the same family, but not the same species as the plant from China. C.A. Bruce later claimed that 'he was the first European who ever penetrated the forests and visited the tea tracts in Suddiya'. However, this claim was later challenged by Lieutenant Charlton, who had served in Assam. In 1831, eight years later, he dispatched complete tea plants including seeds and flowers, which were identified with certainty as the same species as the China tea plant by the botanical authority, at Calcutta.

Maniram Divan, Bruce's informant about tea bushes in Assam, was then in the official service of the king of Assam, Raja Purender Singla. However, the British deposed the latter in 1838 and Maniram Divan joined the Assam Company as a land agent. He left after six years, and opened two gardens himself in Jorhat, upper Assam. He also kept close contacts with the deposed king. The consequences; in retrospect, seem inevitable. Due to his loyalties to the king, he became involved with some leaders of the Revolt of 1857. This cost him dearly as the next year he was hanged by the British after being convicted by a kangaroo court. But Maniram's role in guiding Bruce in locating the tea tracts of the Singhpos and thus helping him, has not been adequately recognised.

In 1834, when the East India Company's monopoly over the Chinese tea trade was abolished by the British Government, the Company turned its attention to India more seriously. Lord William Bentinck, the Governor-General taking the time honoured first step, proceeded to form a committee to investigate the possibilities of growing tea in India. The Committee included seven agents of the East India Company, three Calcutta dealers, and two eminent Indians. The Tea Committee sent G.J. Gordon to China to bring back plants and seeds. However, he discovered that his task was not at all easy as the Chinese had no intention of letting foreigners get hold of the secrets or even the seeds of their valuable industry.

Despite this, however, Gordon managed to send some seeds and these were grown in Assam. But they soon sickened and died and it became quite apparent that the Chinese plants were not suitable for the Indian soil and climate. At the same time some indigenous Assamese plants grown from seeds gathered by C.A. Bruce flourished and grew well. This development, in 1836, was an important one and C.A. Bruce became a central figure in the local development of tea culture for several years.

Bruce was an ex-Lieutenant in the British Royal Navy. He was one of the first Europeans to penetrate the forests in the region of Suddiya. He was made superintendent of the Government Tea Forests, and with his knowledge of the district and its inhabitants, he was the ideal man for this job. In the next few years he did some fine pioneering work. Tea was found to have been grown and planted in groups in many parts of the Brahmaputra Valley. Bruce identified and mapped over 120 such tea tracts where the local people had cultivated tea. He worked in the jungles and lived in a crude *basha* or hut where he made extensive notes on the ways of cultivating the tea plant which were invaluable for those who followed.

The early pioneers in Assam had little idea of how to grow or process the tea. During the days of the China tea trade, the East India Company was simply the buyer and was thus not involved with the cultivation or processing of tea that it bought. The tea was collected by the Chinese tea merchants, in distant villages, sorted and refined at tea centres. Eventually the tea was brought to Canton and sold in lots.

In 1848, Robert Fortune, an Englishman, had visited the Chinese tea gardens, disguised as a Chinese merchant, and made notes on the growing and processing of tea. While this was of some help, the early pioneers in India had only vague ideas of the proper way in which to cultivate the plant and treat the leaf and, consequently, they had many failures in their efforts to grow tea. They brought in some Chinese who supposedly had some knowledge of planting and treating the leaf, but they often found that the Chinese experts were as ignorant as themselves. However, they persisted in their efforts and by trial and error met with some mixed success.

The first tea, however, to be shipped to England was plucked from the indigenous wild bushes growing in

Assam and, probably, originally planted by the Singhpo tribesmen. It was manufactured in the Chinese manner by the imported Chinese experts. Although the quantity supplied was small and totalled only 12 chests, the Tea Committee was justifiably proud. Being aware of the great care taken by the Chinese 'in preventing consignments of tea being shipped on board vessels that have cargoes consisting of articles of strong flavour and which are known to be injurious to the delicate and fugacious aroma of tea', and since much of the cargo of the UK bound ships at that time apparently consisted of ox-hide, each chest was put in a soldered tin case. Despite this only eight chests were received in a fit condition for sale. The tea brokers, who tasted the tea, described it as burnt and rather harsh but, nevertheless, competitive with China brands, and it was sold at a very good average of 20 shillings per pound, a very good price denoting not its true value but rather its novelty.

However, the British were still accustomed to the Chinese tea industry and the tea-drinking consumer of China. Thus when they first started auctioning of Assam tea they continued to be graded as Hysons, Gunpowders, Congous and Souchongs following the Chinese grades. It was not until the 1860s that the Pekoes and Orange Pekoes and other distinctive Indian tea designations were advertised openly on the wholesale market. By that time, of course, Indian teas were firmly entrenched.

The early planters of tea in India were resourceful and energetic British individuals who penetrated the jungles and after much hard work established plantations. It was only later that the large public companies followed. The first planters opened up inaccessible hill tracts, dense jungles and malaria-infested marshes to create the first

plantations that have grown into the giant estates of today.
They rode on elephants, horses or sat on bullock carts
or were carried in a variety of slung chairs along the
rude tracts and then took to walking to climb the crags
and cliffs. The early British planters were the first to
make clearings in forests infested with elephants and bison,
tigers and leopards, wild boars and wild dogs. They also
built grass huts to live in. They planted the first nurseries
and raised the first crops as they went on to clear another
block or two.

These pioneers had little capital, but believed that with
industry and enterprise they could earn a comfortable
livelihood, yet few made fortunes. Most of these men
had hardly any qualifications, but they were men of
action. There were exceptions, of course, and there was
one planter I read about who used to sit under a tea
bush and read the *New Testament* in Greek. 'Their
isolation sometimes bred eccentricity, in others an
excessive love of alcohol.'

The Tea Board of India has described below the
opening up of the High Range in Kerala, but it is
obvious that the travails of early planters in Assam were
similar to those in south India.

'The first among them was J.D. Munro who, in 1877,
bought from the Poonait Raja of Auchanaad (a tributary
of the Maharaja of Travancore) the main portion of what
is now the High Range. These pioneers first began to
tame the virgin lands and forests to the needs of man.
They tried many crops – coffee, cinchona, sisal, cardamom
– before they found in tea a means to make these
reluctant hills productive. The workers faced many
dangers – wild elephants, diseases, floods and landslides –
before their successors were in a position to bring the

tools of the best available technology to the
developmental task which increased its tempo after 1895,
when business houses took over from individual pioneers.
The jungle valleys were increasingly cleared and planted;
roads were opened to all parts of the district, the almost
insuperable difficulties of transport were met with
increasing efficiency first by bullock carts and ropeway
(500 bullocks were at one time engaged in the transport
of tea) then by a monorail system, later by two feet
gauge light railway and finally, by a combination of
ropeways, lorries and tractors.'

In Assam the local Ahoms had ruled for 600 years
except for a brief interlude of 26 years when the state
came under the Mughal sway, after which it reverted to
the Ahoms. In the early 1800s, there were constant
conflicts between the Ahoms and the Burmese. The
British Government intervened through the first Burmese
War, and by 1823 much of Assam was under British
authority. The whole state came under the British by
1838, as a result of which the East India Company
became an instrument of government and not of trade.
It, therefore, handed over its budding tea enterprise to a
strictly commercial concern.

In 1838, the Assam Company was formed amidst
much enthusiasm and excitement. Prosperous citizens,
eager for quick money, rushed to buy its shares. But in
the early years there was mismanagement and a total lack
of cost consciousness. Poor tea was produced which had
no takers in London. The Company suffered considerable
losses and a large number of shareholders lost their
money.

The Assam Company made a request for the services
of C.A. Bruce, and he duly joined the Company in 1840.

One of the first problems he encountered was, to say the least, unusual in corporate affairs. Bruce had to abandon several tea tracts in the first year of operations, because the Assamese of a district rose in rebellion and massacred the British Colonel and his entire garrison.

Trouble also arose from the Assam Company's attempts to import labour. The Assamese were described as 'very lazy', but the real fact was that they would only work on tea plantations when they were not cultivating or harvesting their own rice fields. The Company initially decided to employ Chinese labour. But there was trouble, and as a Company report quoted by H.A. Antrobus in the *History of the Assam Company* states, 'A large number of Chinese labourers were brought from Singapore, but they were selected without discretion. Every man with a pigtail was supposed to be qualified to cultivate, manipulate and prepare tea.' This effort was, therefore, a total failure and the Chinese were described as 'turbulent, obstinate and rapacious'. They were, finally, sent back to Calcutta and deported.

In desperation the Company employed Europeans as 'paid recruiters'. A certain W.S. Stewart agreed to collect labourers from Ranchi in Bihar, at a commission of Rs 2 per head for men and Re 1 for women and children, plus a handsome monthly salary. For several months Stewart drew his salary, but did not move from Calcutta. His excuse was that he was suffering from poor health, and also that he was being cheated by a Company foreman. It is not clear whether he ever reached Ranchi but, nevertheless, drew large sums of money from the Company for wages, feeding and transport of the huge gang of labourers who were eagerly awaited in Assam. En route he drew money for the purchase of 700 blankets for the workers who were on the march with him. Finally, several months later he arrived at Devagunj in Assam, alone without any labourers of any description. The lamentable and improbable news he gave was that as a result of an outbreak of cholera among them, the whole batch of 700 men had absconded the night before. He even took the precaution of producing some sort of a medical certificate from the Civil Surgeon corroborating his story. In the Assam Company's Calcutta Board Reports for 1840-41, it is stated that the total cost of Stewart's recruiting operations which produced no labourers was Rs 10,727, no mean sum in those days!

Stewart was not an exception and Antrobus quotes another report of the Assam Company about a trusted Senior Assistant, Alexander Hart, who had been with the Company since its inception. Besides the mundane job of producing tea he had devoted much of his time to the far more profitable and exotic exercise of trading in elephants on his own account. Mr Hart and his elephants were also dismissed.

These instances of chicanery were possible because supervision was difficult due to lack of communication. The tea gardens could be 100 miles apart, and the only method of transport was by elephants through the dense jungle.

Elephants were always a temptation to European assistants who bought them from the local tribesmen and then sold them. It cost virtually nothing to keep an elephant, so by selling one for Rs 250 to Rs 300 the Assistant was able to augment substantially his meagre salary of Rs 50 to Rs 100 per month. By the end of World War I, the salaries had improved and the young men started on a salary of Rs 250 a month though an assistant on a smaller estate was still paid Rs 100. They were also given six months home leave every five years on half pay. The one-way fare to England was £18 per person. On the other hand, the cost of living was cheap. A whole sheep was Rs 5, a chicken about 35 pices, and a bottle of Scotch for Rs 3 only!

Elephants played a major role in the early tea gardens. In fact, the early planters could not get by without the help of elephants. Assam at the time was infested with tigers and other wild animals and even though an elephant could do only three or four miles an hour, it provided some safety for getting around. It could push its way through the thick jungle and was ideal for fording the numerous rivers and swamps. Feeding the elephants was not a cause for worry as the jungle was a splendid feeding ground.

The affairs of the Assam Company went from bad to worse, and a contemporary critic writing in 1863 stated, 'In one place the labour was insufficient – the cultivation in another was bad – the soil was not selected with reference to the requirement of the plant, in a third – the superintendence in a fourth was inefficient – ignorance everywhere was rampant – and to crown all the tea, when manufactured, was pronounced by the London brokers to be bad.' The Board even considered the case for liquidation of the company.

The appointment of Stephen Mornay as Superintendent did much to turn around the Company affairs. He cut down the European staff and reduced the wages of labour from Rs 3.8 annas a month to Rs 3. Out of chaos and disorganisation he brought the gardens to a state of economic production. His brother, Henry

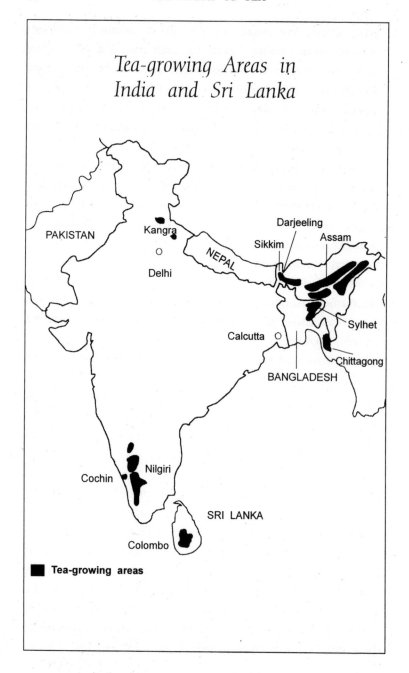

Tea-growing Areas in
India and Sri Lanka

Mornay, who rose to be the Managing Director, continued the sterling work in resuscitating the Company. Under his regime more effective methods of tea cultivation were employed greatly increasing the yield. At the same time the treatment of the plucked leaf was improved so that the quality of tea manufactured became more acceptable.

Soon after, George Williamson, perhaps one of the greatest of the tea pioneers, appeared on the Assam scene. With the further improvements he wrought, the apparently doomed Assam Company was transformed into a profitable operation. On some of the estates the Company had persisted with the China plant or *jat*. Williamson was certain that the root of the trouble was the 'cursed China *jat*' and he decided to replace this with selected Assam *jat*. *Jat* or *zaat* is a Hindi word meaning caste. The company directors were alarmed at first, but Williamson was proved right as the Assam *jat* was better suited to local conditions. In 1856, the Company was able to pay a dividend of nine per cent.

Much has been written about the Assam Company so far since it was the only one in the field. In 1859, the Jorhat Company was founded and flourished as the second public company in the tea industry in Assam. As work progressed the amount of tea produced in the north-east increased rapidly year after year. The Assam Clearance Act was passed in 1854, which gave up to 3,000 acres of prime land to any European planter who promised to cultivate tea for export.

Conditions for local labour who worked on the plantations were harsh and inhuman. They worked very long hours without respite and without health care, and their ranks were decimated by disease. A labourer who left the garden could be sent to prison. Absenteeism was punished by flogging. About one-third of the plantation's employees died on site, for they were underfed, housed on swampy, mosquito-infested ground, and worked in monsoon rain. The workers shivered in thatched mud-walled huts, whole families to a room, the occasional blanket provided by the Company to be shared. They had little money and barely any clothes. They lived from day to day, spending what little money they had. Women and children were subject to the same kind of treatment as the men. These conditions could only be imposed under colonialism.

Two major developments in the latter half of the 19th century altered the shape of commerce in India. These were the opening of the Suez Canal in 1869, and the advances in the railway system in the last decades of the century. Both these developments greatly accelerated the expansion of overseas markets for Indian tea. Another result was the establishment of Calcutta as the commercial capital of the East, with interests based on tea, jute and indigo.

Tea, gradually, spread to other parts of the country with plantations being established in Darjeeling (West Bengal), in the foothills of the Himalaya, and further eastwards in what is known as the Dooars, the Nilgiris or the Blue Mountains in south India, and Chittagong and Sylhet in what is now Bangladesh. Small gardens also came up in the Kangra Valley and Dehra Doon in the north-west of India.

Darjeeling, a hill station in the Himalaya, is situated at an altitude of 7,000 feet. It produces the world's finest tea which has often been called the 'champagne of tea'.

Its fine quality and delicate bouquet enables it to command a premium over all other teas. As a 'tea man' and a lover of Darjeeling tea, I wonder whether champagne should not more appropriately be called the Darjeeling of wines! Darjeeling commands a magnificent view of the snowy ranges in Bhutan and Nepal, dominated by the Kanchenjunga (28,146 feet), the third highest peak in the world and believed by some to be the abode of the God Shiva.

The tea is grown at various altitudes ,up to 6,500 feet, although the average is between 3,000 and 4,000 feet. The China plant, although unsuccessful in its trials on the plains of Assam, was found to be more suited to these higher elevations around Darjeeling. The panorama of tea gardens in this mountainous area is magnificent. The closely-grown tea plants form an unending green carpet which hug the dramatic slopes of the Himalaya slinking down the valleys and climbing to the peaks. Plants are sometimes terraced on a 45 degree incline where the plucking can be only done by hand. As machines can never venture there, this is a permanent guarantee of quality.

The Darjeeling tea district is a small one with only 61 gardens of note. Only a limited amount of tea is grown here, but because of its premium image the so-called Darjeeling tea sold around the world is many times more than is grown in Darjeeling. The usual method is to put a small percentage of Darjeeling tea into the blend with the rest being the more common teas from other parts of India or Sri Lanka. The label, however, would describe it as Darjeeling tea or compromise by calling it a Darjeeling blend. This is not unlike the situation of Black Label scotch whisky – more of it is sold in New

Delhi than is produced in Scotland. Both Nepal and
Sikkim, the latter a small state in India, lie in the same
general areas as Darjeeling and also produce some fine-
quality tea.

Tea is also grown in north-west India in the Kangra
Valley in the beautiful mountain state of Himachal
Pradesh, which lies adjacent to Kashmir. The main tea
area is Palampur at the foothills of the Himalaya. The
Kangra Valley is connected with the Kullu Valley,
renowned for its apple orchards. The area planted under
tea is small. Being at a high elevation this region is also
planted with the China *jat*. The leaf is made into green
tea and the product is sent to Amritsar for distribution
mainly into Kashmir.

Some 2,400 kilometres from the Himalaya foothills lie
the tea and coffee growing regions of south India. Tea
here is grown on the southern slopes of the Western
Ghats, the Nilgiri hills, the High Range or Kanan Devans,
Wynaad and southern Kerala. Some of these are regions
of great beauty. The tea districts are located at elevations
ranging from sea level to 5,000 feet and, perhaps, the
highest tea in the world is planted in parts of the Kanan
Devans at 8,000 feet. South India produces roughly a
quarter of Indian tea, the balance being from north-east
India. South Indian tea is light with a delicate flavour. In
1948, a tea market with auctions was opened in Cochin
and in 1963 in Conoor.

It is interesting to note that in the early days, tea in
south India was very much a subsidiary crop, which
counted for little compared to the coffee plantations.
However, in some areas when the coffee industry declined
tea began to be cultivated.

For the pioneer planter in south India, it was a fight

against great odds. With the help of his band of workers, he first had to fell the thick primeval forest in order to carve out a clearing. Such clearings where the seeds were planted formed the new estates. The pioneer planter had to constantly fight diseases, the heavy monsoon rains, and ward off wild animals as well. It was a ceaseless fight. The early plantations were established in the mid-1800s and Sir Percival Griffith's quotation from the *Planting Opinion* graphically describes the hardships and travails the early planters had to face.

'It was with great difficulty that the gardens were opened out; the dense forest swarmed with elephants and other wild beasts, as well as smugglers (*moplahs*) going through with smuggled sandalwood from the Mysore province. There was great scarcity of labour . . . The assistants lived on estates in what can only be described as shacks, while the manager lived in slightly less discomfort in a traveller's bungalow six miles from the first estate.

It was with difficulty that provisions were to be got; bread, meat, and sugar from Ootacamund . . . coarse rice and at times horse gram were brought. This was the coarse food that the superintendent and their men had to subsist on and be contented . . . They looked very sickly suffering from malarial fever and enlargement of the spleen . . . The medicine that they were taught to take was Tartar emetic and during high fever and headache a couple of horse leeches were applied to the temples until they drew blood and gave relief.'

The hill station of Ootacamund or Ooty situated over 6,000 feet was a place for recuperation and recreation. The cool air of the Nilgiri mountains is most healing after the heat and dust of the plains. The Ooty Club, housed in a mansion with a handsome driveway, was originally built in 1832. It is to this day an excellent institution, with its manicured lawns, well-maintained club building and the sparkling silver in the dining room.

The auctioning of tea started in Calcutta in 1861. Much of the tea business was handled by old established agency houses around Clive Street, Calcutta. Many of these, albeit as new incarnations in Indian hands, are familiar even today. Duncan Brothers, Williamson Magor, Balmer Lawrie, Gillander Arbuthnot, Carrit Moran, Shaw Wallace, J. Thomas, James Finlay, and so on.

Since the independence of India in 1947, most of these British companies have sold out to Indians. The Assam Company, Jorhat Company, etc., are all in Indian hands. One of the world's largest tea-growing companies, Tata Tea, is a totally Indian owned company. In the year 2000, Tata Tea acquired the Tetley Group, thus making Tata Tetley the world's second largest tea conglomerate with Unilever, which has bought out both blockbusters Brooke Bond and Lipton in recent years, being the largest. The Tata Tetley brands now cover 44 countries and also open up enormous possibilities for the Tatas. There is a David and Goliath angle to the entire transaction. Tata Tea is by far the smaller company and its turnover of Rs 885 crores is small compared to the Tetley's turnover, which analysts reckon, have racked up an annual turnover of Rs 2,240 crores. This is a path-breaking acquisition for an Indian company as it provides it a global opportunity.

Production in the last several decades has been increasing rapidly, and India now is by far the largest tea producer in the world. In 1900, India's tea production was small, but rose to 177 million kilograms in 1930 to

577 million kilograms in 1980 to 750 million kilograms in 1995. A truly spectacular record, achieved through higher yields, increasing acreage under tea and by cultivation in non-traditional areas. India's target for the year 2000 was 1,000 million kilograms. Sri Lanka is a poor second with a production of 191 million kilograms in 1980.

The tea industry in India was originally established to supply tea to the British market. During the latter half of the 19th century, India's domestic consumption was negligible. Even as late as 1954, it was a mere 70 million kilograms of a total Indian crop of 217 million kilograms.

However, since independence there has been a tremendous spurt in Indian consumption mainly because of the increasing prosperity of the consumer as well as the expanding distribution network of the leading packaged tea companies like Brooke Bond India, Lipton India and Tata Tea, which have extended their network from the urban areas into the burgeoning rural markets. This has resulted in a retention of 70 per cent of the total crop of 750 million kilograms in 1995, within the country for domestic consumption, making it the world's largest consumer of tea. However, with this large percentage being consumed within India, one might have imagined that it had hindered the country's efforts in exporting tea to the world market. But it has proved to the contrary.

Domestic consumption, in fact, has proved a valuable support to the Indian producers. This huge domestic tea market has protected the Indian producers from the vagaries of the world tea market. During periods of over supply in the world market, international prices drop sharply and there is a general depression. The internal

Indian market, however, provides a cushion to the Indian producers against such international depressions. Without this steady support of the internal market, the Indian production would not have been the world's largest today. Sri Lanka and Africa, not having the safety valve of a large domestic market, are more dependent on the international situation.

5

Sri Lanka – The Isle of Tea

Off the southern tip of India, Sri Lanka (formerly Ceylon) is a small island 400 kilometres from north to south and 200 kilometres at its widest from east to west. It is mountainous in the south expanding into a wide plain towards the north. The soil is fertile and the vegetation very luxuriant with fruit trees, coconut palms, and vivid green rice fields immersed in water. Kandy, the last capital of the Sinhalese kings, lies in the foothills. Beyond Kandy, the forest-covered mountains, interspersed with a carpet of rich green tea bushes, rise to 6,000 feet.

The Sri Lankans or Sinhalese are descendants of colonists from the Ganges Valley who settled on the island about the 6th century BC and established the Sinhalese dynasty. Sri Lankans had a developed civilisation several centuries before Christ. Rome used to trade with Sri Lanka with her ships following the monsoon across

the ocean. The British deposed the 186th and last king
of Sri Lanka in 1815. As a result of many generations of
war, Tamils from south India occupied the northern
region of the island. In the last century many more
Tamils followed as immigrant labour.

Sri Lanka has had four great plantation crops which
have been important on the world stage. The first of
these was cinnamon which was indigenous to the island.
The stripping of cinnamon bark in the jungle had long
been a hereditary occupation among the Sinhalese. The
plantations near Colombo came later. Coffee was,
probably, introduced into the island by Arab traders and
had been grown on small holdings till the English tried
it out on a commercial scale about 1840. Huge areas of
forest were cleared for the coffee plantations and
elephants were very useful for this purpose. Land at that
time was available around Kandy at £1 per acre and for
even less further in the interior. While this may sound
more than reasonable, what in fact the planter bought
was dense jungle, which involved clearing and burning
the trees before he could establish a nursery and plant
the land with coffee. He could look forward to no
income for the next four or five years while expenses
mounted. All this required not only capital, but also a
spirit of adventure and guts. Coffee in Sri Lanka
prospered and not only was the quality as good as any
in the world, but the production also increased manifold
and was second to Brazil, the world's largest producer.
However, disaster struck in 1869 when coffee rust
(*Hamelera vastatrix*) appeared and laid waste the
country's coffee plantations. Hundreds of coffee estates
lay abandoned and the labour force remained unpaid.
Planters who survived this disaster turned first to

cinchona (the bark of this tree is used to make quinine). They cultivated cinchona on a huge scale, and by 1883 there were 64,000 acres under cinchona. But this proved their undoing and due to heavy overproduction the world market collapsed. After this second disaster, showing great courage, the erstwhile coffee planters turned cinchona planters finally turned to tea. The pioneer was James Taylor, who had successfully tried both cinchona and later tea at Loolecondera estate where he started growing and manufacturing tea for local consumption; the year was 1867. Taylor was an unusual man. His only interest in life was the Loolecondera estate. He was 16 years old when he signed on for Sri Lanka. He never saw his native Scotland again, but throughout his life he wrote letters to his father, a humble wheelwright, giving a unique description of the daily life of a planter in the mid-1800s. He never owned the estate, but did such a splendid job that the estate tea became famous. He never left the estate in all his years in Sri Lanka and seems to have enjoyed his solitude. Ultimately, there came a time when the large corporations based in Britain, forced out the smaller plantations like Loolecondera and Taylor like other planters was dismissed. He refused to quit the estate despite orders to do so, which posed quite a problem for the company. Not long afterwards he suddenly died at the age of 57 on his beloved Loolecondera. There is no record of where Taylor was buried, but I do hope it was on the estate.

British planters were a tough lot and they increased the acreage dramatically by working hard during the next few years. In 1880, the figure had reached an astonishing

34 million pounds (15½ million kilograms). A tremendous stride in a single decade! This was, however, still a modest share of the world market, which from figures available for 1884, had reached a level of 174 million pounds (79 million kilograms). Competitors who were, of course, China and India were on their guard against the entry of another formidable rival.

It was about this time that a decline set in in the import of Chinese tea into Britain. While tea in India and Sri Lanka was being grown on well organised plantations, with efficient cultivation and manufacture resulting in consistent and good quality, the Chinese tea production was still a small farmer operation and collection of the leaf was arduous and its processing inept. The packing was also deficient, and thus the tea that arrived in England used to be in a stale condition. In short, China had not moved with the times and it was no longer competitive. Chinese tea sales peaked at 136 million pounds (62 million kilograms) in 1879 after which there was a sensational decline. Competitors like India and Sri Lanka gained significantly, more so Sri Lanka, as its tea industry was still in its early stages and the Chinese debacle gave it a timely stimulus.

Sri Lanka also had the advantage of not going through the teething problems which the Indian tea industry had. By now there was enough experience of growing and manufacturing tea in the Assam tea gardens, and the early Sri Lankan planters could take advantage of this. Their techniques of cultivation and processing had not been perfected, but the British planters in Sri Lanka were innovative and not loath to experiment and with the industry looking up there was much enthusiasm and optimism. The island's planters experimented with the

China *jat* as well as with the Assam and south India *jats*. The manufacture of tea had also been mechanised in India to some extent and Sri Lanka also profited a great deal from these advances.

The success of Sri Lankan tea also owed much to the ideal terrain and climate of the island. Like south India, Sri Lanka had been graced by both the south-west and the north-east monsoons. This tropical downpour totalled 100 to 150 inches in the tea-growing areas and resulted in rapid and luxuriant growth. In addition, Sri Lanka tea was cultivated at various altitudes: low-grown (up to 2,000 feet), mid-grown (2,000 to 4,000 feet) and high-grown (above 4,000 feet). Almost 70 per cent of the tea in Sri Lanka is grown on hillsides that are 2,000 feet and above. Each altitude produced tea which was perceptibly different. The high-grown tea has a fine flavour comparable to the Nilgiri tea of south India as well as the esteemed but different fragrance of the Darjeeling tea of north India. Thus while Sri Lankan tea was in a separate category from the strong Assam tea and, therefore, not in direct competition, it was a clear alternative for the mild and pleasant tea from China, which because of its deterioration was now vulnerable to the Sri Lankan variety. Most of the tea that we drink is a blend of different types of compatible teas. The blend could be made from teas from different gardens or even from distant regions and countries. In these blends, Sri Lanka tea could easily substitute for China tea.

Finally, Sri Lanka had a significant advantage in growing other major plantation crops in the country, particularly coffee. This had given the island an infrastructure in terms of ports, roads, transport, etc., which were well suited for the high volume exports of

tea. Unlike Assam the availability of labour was also not
a problem. The Sinhalese, like the Assamese, did not
relish plantation work, but here the gap was filled up by
the hard-working Tamils from south India, who happily
settled down on the estates. Their arrival in earlier
centuries as a result of wars fought and the 19th century
migration as labour, swelled their numbers on the island
and this created problems of its own for Sri Lanka.

With all these advantages, Sri Lankan tea made
spectacular progress, and by 1890 its exports to the major
market, Britain, had impressed the tea trade as well as
alerted competitors – China and India. And then suddenly
one of those developments took place which took
everyone by surprise – Sri Lankan tea became the fashion,
the social style in Britain. In the last decade of the 19th
century what is described as Ceylon fever caught on.
Assam tea had taste and strength, but the British
consumer discovered a subtle flavour in the Sri Lankan
leaf and embraced it with an ardour and excitement
which was quite extraordinary. The island's name was at
a premium and gardens tried to cash in on this by
marketing teas in Britain, unblended and under the estate
name. For packet tea companies, the magic word on
their labels became Ceylon. Some packagers who could
not buy enough Sri Lankan tea at an economic price,
would blend it heavily with tea from India or China, but
would still label it as Ceylon while others, to keep out
of trouble, would use the ambiguous term Ceylon Blend.
In more recent times such problems of controversial
branding have also afflicted Darjeeling tea for which
demand has always exceeded supply.

The boom in Sri Lankan tea culminated in the well-
recorded Golden Tips auction of 1891. Normally two

leaves and a bud in between are plucked from the tea bush. In this case, the buds were sorted separately by hand and the leaves were left out. These buds in the case of high quality tea turn golden and hence the name Golden Tips. The producers and agents went on a promotional blitz, and built up an exaggerated mystique about the high quality of Golden Tips. For a short time ridiculous prices were paid for this tea. In January 1891, the price paid was £4.7sh per pound at the Mincing Lane auctions. Buyers competed with each other and put in incredible bids. Over the next few months the price zoomed to £17 per pound, then to £25, to £30 and finally, to a stupendous £36 in August, 1891. Considering the value of money 100 years ago, this was an incredible price for tea. Apparently realising that such madness could lead to ruin, when Golden Tips came up for sale in December it was ignored and prices reverted to saner levels. The Golden Tips frenzy had ended.

In the 1880s and 1890s, stocking good quality tea was a must for a retailer as it was one of the main items on the consumer's shopping list. The reputation of the grocer in the neighbourhood was literally determined by the quality of tea that he stocked. Interestingly, Arthur Brooke who established one of the largest tea companies in the world, Brooke Bond Limited, started life about this time by opening the doors of his first shop in Manchester selling only tea, coffee and sugar for cash over the counter. It is difficult to visualise today, where shops stock hundreds of grocery items, how they could stock just three items and yet prosper and do well. Arthur Brooke was typical of such grocers of the time. Tea then represented the loss leader of modern times, which is used the world over to entice customers into the shop with the aim that though the customer will come for the price advantage on the loss leader he or she will end up buying so much else. This importance of tea in the retail trade at this particular juncture coincided with the fashion for Sri Lankan tea and gave an additional fillip to the progress of the island's tea industry.

Sir Thomas Lipton also started life with a single grocery shop. Ten years later, in 1890, he headed a chain of three hundred shops and ended by establishing a worldwide business empire. Lipton will always be associated with three things – tea, Ceylon and yachting. In 1890, when Lipton was 40 and already a millionaire and his shops were famous for their hams and cheeses, he entered the tea trade. Tea made Lipton a billionaire. He made money so fast that he lost count of it, and this was at a time when income tax stood at 5 per cent. His name was closely allied with the success of Ceylon tea, but the master propagandist that he was, his role was clearly exaggerated by himself and his public relations men. In 1890, he arrived at the Grand Oriental Hotel in Colombo amidst much fanfare, and announced that he would be the largest tea garden owner on the island. This investment in land was a pretty shrewd move because after the coffee blight, plantation land in Sri Lanka was going at ridiculously low prices, as half-ruined planters were desperate to sell their land. 'You can buy estates for a song,' Lipton was told. He snapped up 3,000 acres for £20,000 though the figure of his investment in Sri Lanka was inflated and published as around £100,000. This venture into tea enabled Lipton to bypass the auctions at Mincing Lane and directly channel the tea from his estates to his numerous retail outlets in Britain, thereby not only increasing his profit margins, but reducing the price to the consumer as well.

Lipton's plan was to sell worldwide, blends of good quality Ceylon tea, attractively packaged, at the lowest possible prices. At the same time he would support all blends with heavy advertising. 'Advertise,' he would say, 'advertise all you can. But make sure that what you advertise is good.' His slogan: 'Direct from the tea garden to the teapot' had a unique appeal of freshness for the consumer. A splendid marketing strategy and a sure recipe for success!

He publicised his Sri Lanka estates and gave the impression that the tea came from his own gardens, but if every packet bearing a Lipton label had come from his own property, he would have needed to own half the island! In point of fact, tea from many other estates had to be blended and only a small part of the tea that went into Lipton's packets came from his own estates. People muttered and complained that Ceylon was no longer a British colony but a Lipton colony.

Lipton's faith in advertising was quite remarkable. When he started his first grocery shop and could not afford to advertise, he bought two of the fattest pigs in the market. He tied pink and blue ribbons round their tails and had them driven all over the small town by a gentleman in a cutaway coat and top hat. On the pigs' sides was painted, 'I am going to Lipton's, the best shop in town, for Irish bacon.'

Throughout his career Lipton remained a great believer in advertising. Once on a voyage to Sri Lanka, Lipton's ship ran aground somewhere in the Red Sea and some of the cargo had to be thrown overboard. Lipton, the incorrigible businessman, persuaded one of the engineers

to cut him a stencil and while the other passengers were
hurrying to the lifeboats, Lipton, never a man to lose an
opportunity, was busy stenciling 'Drink Lipton Tea' on
such of the cargo as was likely to float in the shallow
water and be salvaged. Though he lost his luggage in the
Red Sea, this incident received much publicity, which was
ample compensation. Lipton pulled off his biggest publicity
stunt when a town in Canada was named after him.

Having reached the height of success and fame,
Thomas Lipton, finally, devoted himself to his passion,
which was sailing. He became one of the most famous
challengers for the America Cup. He competed several
times in his life, in his youth, in middle age and even
in old age, but it was one of his major regrets that he
never won. All his superb racing yachts were named
Shamrock. The British public avidly followed Lipton's
exploits who, despite his lack of success in the America
Cup, remained the tea gentleman. In Sri Lanka,
however, he was known as Tea Tom. P.J. Banyard
mentions that by virtue of his enthusiasm for yachting
he became a friend of King Edward VII, although not
everyone approved of such relaxation of social discipline.
Kaiser Wilhelm II was distressed that, 'My uncle had
gone boating with his grocer.' But the fact was that
Lipton was not merely a grocer who had made money.
He was a dashing man, a clever man who had travelled
much and had a strong sense of Irish humour. From the
very moment he was presented to the King, he
comported himself as one thoroughly accustomed to the
presence of royalty. Once when King Edward referring
to the Order of Knight Commander remarked, 'Lipton,
I think I shall give you an order shortly.' Lipton
jocularly retorted, 'That is exceedingly kind of Your

Majesty. It will do me a lot of good in my business. I shall have a price list sent to Your Majesty at once.'

Another story about Lipton was that despite the backing of King Edward VII, the well-known tycoon was denied membership of the exclusive Royal Yacht Squadron in Cowes because he had begun his career selling ham. Lipton was, however, admitted 30 years later. On hearing the news, he sardonically enquired, 'Which club did you say and whereabouts is it?'

By 1900, Sri Lanka had become one of the world's three biggest tea producers. India's production stood at 192 million pounds (87 million kilograms), followed by China with 185 million pounds (84 million kilograms) and Sri Lanka with 149 million pounds (68 million kilograms) per year. Today India is by far the largest producer of tea in the world with the production of 750 million kilograms. But unlike India which consumes more than half its own production, Sri Lanka exports almost all its tea and thus its exports are pretty close to those of India. The auctioning of tea started in Colombo as early as 1883. Much of the tea business was handled in Colombo fort by old established agency houses like J.M. Robertson, George Steuart, Mackwood & Lee Hedges.

Tea has received a great deal of attention from the Sri Lankan Government as the country practically lives off its tea which accounted for 70 per cent of its total export revenue. The Government of Sri Lanka has over several years undertaken to advertise and promote the country's tea in the international markets. This effort first started in 1887, when cooperative advertising for the tea industry as a whole was undertaken and has continued effectively to the present day.

Sri Lanka nationalised the tea industry and after 1972

brought in wide-ranging land reforms covering 600,000 acres of plantation. Wages for plantation labour, most of whom are Tamils, have also been improved. Since the British first opened up plantations with indentured labour in the 1870s, wages remained at subsistence level, but now significant improvements have been made in wage scales. In collaboration with the World Bank and other international agencies, new housing is being built for plantation workers and 'the degrading barrack-like line rooms, a hangout from British times are being restructured into roomy cottages'. Other educational and social welfare measures are also being adopted which will greatly improve their quality of life.

6

Tea in Africa and other Countries

The development of tea in Africa is a comparatively recent venture. Although production of tea started in the last few decades of the 19th century, commercial results of importance were not achieved till the mid-20th century. Since then progress has been rapid; and today Africa is an important producer on the world stage. In fact, it poses a challenge to the traditional tea producers of Asia.

Initially and significantly Brooke Bond, UK, thought of opening tea gardens in Africa as part of a strategic design. In the 1920s, the company anticipated the possibility of political upheaval in India in the coming years, which could disrupt its business worldwide. Brooke Bond must be given credit for such dynamic planning when the possibility of political disruption in India was barely comprehended by the British Government.

Tea-growing Areas in Africa

UGANDA

KENYA

RWANDA

TANZANIA

MALAWI

MOZAMBIQUE

MAURITIUS

ZIMBABWE

Tea-growing areas

Brooke Bond also realised that as the import duty on tea was 1 shilling per pound, if it could produce enough tea locally to supply the east African market, its competitors – obliged to import tea – would lose control of the whole market. This happened within a few years.

Tea in Africa now covers a vast geographical area. It is grown mainly on the eastern side of this great continent and includes Kenya, Uganda, Tanzania, Malawi, Mozambique, Rwanda, Zimbabwe and the distant island of Mauritius. Thus it is planted from the equator where the Kericho area in Kenya is located to 20°S, a distance of about 2,500 kilometres.

After Asia, Africa is the most important continent where tea is grown. British companies opened up the tea-growing areas in Africa in much the same way as they did in India and Sri Lanka.

A paragraph from D. Wainright's *Brooke Bond, A Hundred Years,* tells the story well. 'In 1924, a small piece of land was bought at Limuru and then a larger estate 100 kilometres to the north-west towards Lake Victoria at Kericho . . . Life was tough and primitive. Oxen hauled the carts over the often muddy tracks. The first stage in the development of the estate was clearly the provision of elementary shelter. The two managers in charge of the venture in Kenya built houses, offices, roads and bridges. With their own blasting equipment they quarried stone and made bricks from swamp clay. In the intervals, they tended the tea or supervised local tribesmen who cheerfully cleared many acres of bush. Soon there came the great day when the first pound of Brooke Bond Kenya tea was solemnly packed in a newly built corrugated iron shed that was optimistically designated as the packing factory.' The supply of electricity in the area was limited and erratic. The Brooke Bond engineers, therefore, constructed a hydro-electric plant to provide power for the factory and electric light for the houses.

By such methods, growing tea was established as a major industry in East Africa, but it was only 25 years later in the mid-20th century that it became a sizeable contributor to the economy of Kenya.

The British companies had a major advantage in Africa, because they could take full benefit of their decades of experience in other countries and incorporate the more recent technical advances both in cultivation and in manufacture on the African estates.

Most tea-producing countries have always endeavoured to improve their general efficiency through research. Scientific institutions like Tocklai in Assam, St Coomb's in Sri Lanka, Mlange in Malawi, and Kericho in Kenya, have contributed greatly to technical advances through their valuable research. The advantage has tended to accrue to the more recently planted estates, as in Africa, because tea bushes last over half a century and it is not possible for the older plantations to bring about changes in the short term.

Kenya, the major tea producer on the continent has, like Sri Lanka, two features which enable it to grow good quality tea. These are rainfall and altitude. The main tea-growing areas are the Kenya Highlands, a fairly large area lying between Mount Kenya and Lake Victoria on either side of the great Rift Valley ranging in altitude from 5,000 to 9,000 feet. It has two favourable rainy seasons a year which means that plucking of leaves is possible for most of the year and, therefore, the financial return on plantations is very high.

The Rift Valley viewed a few miles out of Nairobi is quite breathtaking. This great valley formed by two parallel faults between which the earth has sunk rises in Jordan and Israel and embraces the Dead Sea. It then runs south and the Red Sea is a part of this sunken valley. Finally, it turns west into Africa and runs hundreds of kilometres over the continent.

The various tea companies that have financed and developed the tea industry in Kenya have concentrated on breeding high-yielding tea plants which produce good quality tea. On the manufacturing side also they have used some of the most advanced equipment in the world. East Africa and Kenya in particular have, as a result, added a new range of quality to the tea trade. They make a brightly coloured, strong liquoring tea, which is highly valued by blenders.

Alongside tea production by the major companies there is a novel scheme for smallholders which was started in the 1950s and is now run by the Kenya Tea Development Authority. Under this scheme, smallholders have added tea in a mixed farming operation. The area under tea is about one acre in the holding, as that is considered the maximum that a single family can manage efficiently. This experiment has been very successful and more tea is now planted on smallholdings than on the large company estates in Kenya. As we have seen earlier, the system of growing tea by the small farmers in China ultimately proved to be the downfall of China tea, since the production was uneven in quality and the system lacked reliability. It was, therefore, unable to compete with the great plantations of India. However, the Kenya Tea Development Authority has tried to avoid this hazard by ensuring that acceptable plants are sold to smallholders and that cooperative factories are conveniently located to deal with the plucked leaves.

Similar schemes are now working in most other tea-producing African countries, notably Uganda. But care must be taken to see that developing tea through the smallholders does not inhibit development.

Outside Africa, tea is grown in several other countries. In Indonesia, a tropical land outside the range of the monsoons, the conditions are most favourable on the island of Java. Here many estate products became of great commercial importance including rubber, sugar, coffee, tea, tobacco and cinchona, in the last of which Java possessed a near monopoly.

The development of tea in Indonesia started with the Dutch, who arrived there in the early 17th century. It however, became of commercial importance only after 1835, due to the efforts of J.J.L.L. Jacobson, who was in the service of the Dutch East India Company and a great expert on tea at the time. But real success was only obtained in 1878 when Assam seed was first imported and hand manufacture was replaced by machinery. The present tea in Java is practically wholly of the Assam type.

Indonesian teas from Java and Sumatra are well accepted in the international market. They are consistent in quality and appearance throughout the year and the high-grown teas have a flavour somewhat similar to those from corresponding elevations in south India and Sri Lanka. Indonesian tea is also used as fillers, which are added to bring down the price of a blend made up of teas from various countries, without damaging the character and flavour of the blend.

The most northerly estates in the world are in Georgia

on the eastern end of the Black Sea. This is about the same latitude as the north of Italy and the climate is not ideal for tea. A slight variation in rainfall or temperature is far more serious here than in traditional tea climates. Only the small-leaved China variety can grow in these climes. Mechanisation has been extensively introduced and machines straddle the tea bushes. Such tea is satisfactory for everyday use, but not for sophisticated palates used to Darjeeling, Assam, Nilgiri or Sri Lanka teas.

The former Soviet Union greatly expanded tea production in the Caucasus in the 1950s, and production in this area is the fourth largest in the world, although it is far behind India, Sri Lanka and Africa. Georgian tea not being enough to supply its needs, Russia is a keen buyer of the best quality Indian teas, and takes a large proportion of the Darjeeling and good Assams.

Bangladesh is a fairly important tea-growing country. Tea development in Bangladesh took place in the 19th century along with India. As erstwhile East Pakistan, it supplied tea mainly to West Pakistan. But after the India Pakistan War in 1971, Pakistan was forced to surrender and Bangladesh emerged as an independent country, and then diversified its exports to several countries.

In Turkey, tea is grown in the Rize area on the Black Sea only 110 kilometres from Poti, the chief centre of the tea industry in Georgia. There are many other less important tea-growing countries like Iran, Malaysia, etc., but while their tea is quite useful, it is not vital to the big packing companies. Tea is now grown in over 60 countries of the world.

The latest additions to the tea-growing countries are Argentina and to a lesser extent Brazil. In Argentina, the area under tea is rapidly expanding. Neither Brazil nor

Argentina is a tea-drinking country, as Brazil is the largest producer of coffee in the world. Consumers in both these countries naturally prefer coffee. However, they have a convenient market on their doorstep in Chile, which alone among the South American nations drinks significant amounts of tea. Like Indonesia, blenders in London and other centres also use Argentina tea as fillers.

7

Planting and Manufacture of Tea

tea or *Camellia sinensis* is a hardy flowering, evergreen plant grown in several countries. It can be grown over a wide range of climates.

However, one essential requirement for healthy growth is plenty of rainfall. It flourishes best in a jungle atmosphere of heat and humidity. It is an easy plant to grow. But to get a good-quality tea from it is extremely difficult. Soil, aspect, rainfall, elevation, manufacture – are all factors which affect tea in subtle ways. Getting a good-quality tea is often the work of a generation; it does not come quickly.

One normally associates tea plantations with a vast green carpet of well-trimmed lush green tea bushes interspersed with big leafy shade trees stretching across a thousand acres or more of flat plain. Alternately at higher altitudes the green carpet of bushes could closely follow

the contours of the hills, hugging the dramatic curves,
going down the valleys and climbing up to the peaks.
When, however, tea grows wild you can.get a forest of
large trees growing to a height of 30 feet or more. It is
the pruning and plucking, which keeps it at waist level
and gives it the characteristic table-top appearance. There
is reportedly a tea tree in Yunnan, in south-western
China, which is 800 years old with a huge sturdy trunk
and stands 60 feet high. Incredibly, it still produces good
tea which, however, entails climbing to the top of the
tree to pluck the youngest leaves.

There are two ways of planting tea. It can be grown
from seeds or from cuttings by vegetative propagation.
In the former case, the bushes are left unpruned and
allowed to rise to their full height of about 30 to 40
feet. The seeds are taken from these seed bearers and
sown in carefully-prepared nursery beds until they are
strong enough for transplanting to their permanent
position, where they are planted two or three feet apart
in rows, several thousand to an acre. New plants are,
nowadays, more often grown from cuttings by vegetative
propagation. As the cutting produces an absolute replica
or clone of the parent plant, this method has the virtue
of providing uniformity and duplicating the productive
capacity of carefully selected plants.

The saplings take three to seven years to mature into
bushes and if well-cultivated, yield leaves prolifically for
70 to 100 years. The bush is allowed to grow to a
height of three or four feet and then pruned at regular
intervals throughout its life in order to maintain its bush
formation. Regular pruning also encourages the
production of a regular flush of tender leaves and
facilitates plucking.

Proper cultivation requires careful elimination of weed growth, systematic manuring, and application of fertilisers. Shade trees are also grown among the bushes. They bring down the temperature, raise humidity, and replace the nitrogen in the soil. Bushes have to be sprayed with insecticide and carefully watched for signs of ill-health, such as blister blight or one of the root diseases, which are a very serious matter. In an area where tea is cultivated intensively an infection can quickly spread from one plantation to another.

Almost all the tea is plucked by hand and it is a delicate and skilled operation. In most Asian countries, plucking is done by the nimble fingers of women and girls. It is generally said that the smallness, agility and patience of feminine hands are necessary for quantity plucking. With baskets on their backs, silver bracelets on their arms and in their red, yellow and blue saris they make a colourful contrast against the dark green tea plants. They move through the neatly pruned waist-high bushes, their fingers flickering over the plants at astonishing speed. The normal method is to pluck two leaves and a bud, but if the coarser leaves are plucked from lower down the stem, the quantity increases but quality suffers. Depending on world supplies and market trends, producers have to decide whether to concentrate on quality or quantity.

The produce is collected in baskets and is brought to a roadside collection point to be weighed. This is done about twice or thrice a day. In India, a skilled plucker can in an eight-hour-working day, harvest 50,000 stems and gather about 70 to 80 pounds (32-36 kilograms) of green leaves, sufficient to produce about 20 pounds (9 kilograms) of manufactured black tea.

The lack of labour had always been a very serious problem for a long time in Assam. The local villagers were recruited in some numbers, but their main interest were their own paddy fields and, therefore, there was much absenteeism. Later the situation improved when labour from outside Assam was brought in.

When the British were in India, working conditions were harsh. D. Maitland in his *5,000 Years of Tea* says, 'Pluckers and processors served long apprenticeships on subsistence wages and were arrested if they tried to leave the plantation. Cheap labour meant low prices and with tea and bread becoming the mainstay of the British industrial worker's diet, prices had to be kept low. The plantation workers suffered a miserable working life. Indian independence and the formation of tea industry unions have vastly improved the working conditions, with today's pluckers and processors commanding wages higher than those of the national average of labourers.' In Sri Lanka, too, working conditions have dramatically improved in the recent decades.

Tea plucking machines have been experimented with, but they have not been successful. Machines cannot have the same ability as humans to select the correct shoots for plucking.

My acquaintanceship with planters has been limited. But having been the Marketing Director of Brooke Bond India for several years, although I had little professional contact with planters, I have on occasion been to the tea gardens both in Assam and in south India. The planters I met, both British and Indian, have been strangely similar. Perhaps the profession attracts the same sort of individuals. They are what can be described, although not in the strict sense of the term, as Sahibs, white and brown Sahibs. Nowadays, of course, they are mainly the brown Sahibs! They are friendly, gregarious and highly worthy. They are outdoor people, who work hard and play hard. They are not unlike the typical defence services' officers.

Life on the tea estates could be lonely but comfortable. The managers' houses were typical colonial bungalows with large rooms, lofty ceilings and deep, wide verandahs. The furniture was generally old, heavy and comfortable. The verandah invariably had huge, easy, wickerwork chairs with long projecting arms on which you could sling up weary legs. These were aptly known as planters' chairs or more imaginatively the Bombay Fornicators! A number of framed photographs adorned the walls; the table strewn with papers and old magazines. In a row of shelves were untidily stacked a good many books, their bindings stained and ravaged.

A beautiful bungalow I spent some time at was situated in the Nilgiri mountains in south India at the Tiashola estate. One of the gardens here situated at over 8,000 feet, was reputed to be the highest tea garden in the world. The manager's bungalow was set in the estate, but was not far from the great trees of the jungles which covered the hillsides. The contrast between the trim tea bushes and the savage growth of the jungle beyond pleasantly stimulated one's imagination. The view was magnificent; on one side of the ridge on which the bungalow was located, were the Blue Mountains, and on the other a steep precipice, dropping down 7,000 feet to the plains.

There was a profusion of servants, cook, bearer, house boys and gardeners. The manager and his family were well looked after.

Each estate is a little world of its own. It has a school, shops, dispensary, and a temple. The workers and their families may add up to as many as a .thousand. The manager is concerned not only with the growing and manufacture of tea, but also with the personal problems of his workers – their quarrels, financial and family matters, marital disagreements and illnesses.

Tea planters work long hours during the season, and the non-manufacturing periods are spent overhauling the machinery. Up before dawn and a quick cup of tea, the planters take the muster roll, after which they return to their bungalows for breakfast, but by seven o'clock they are back to begin the long stretch in the fields, supervising the work, examining the tea nursery, seeing to the weeding. They return to the bungalow for lunch to deal with the official correspondence waiting for them. Then it is back to the garden and it is only by half past five that work for the day is over. It is a twelve-hour day. It is usual for field assistants to travel around the estates on motorcycles on the numerous narrow paths that criss-cross the extensive gardens.

In a tea area, the club is the hub of social life for all the estates. It may be several miles away, but attendance during weekends is generally good. The club is usually a large pleasant bungalow with extensive grounds. It has a large lounge, a reading room, a billiard room, a small card room, and a couple of tennis courts. There may be some old prints adorning the walls and plenty of well-polished silver in the dining room. The bar is, obviously, the most popular room and the barman knows everyone's preference.

A planter in south India, in the 1920s, recalls, 'Joining a club was quite an expensive item for a "creeper" earning Rs 150 a month. The entry fee of Rs 50 was a must for those who wanted to meet their fellow men on the off day. Senior members arrived in the 'T' model cars or maybe in a tonga – if in the latter, it was an opportunity to show, with pride, the recently purchased pair of bullocks boasting of the price as a car owner might boast of the miles per gallon (4.5 litres). Younger members would ride, syces going ahead with food for their master for the midday meal, and their boys arriving a little later to be on time to serve lunch.'

Another planter said, 'The early members were a spirited lot, whose behaviour sometimes verged on the rowdy and in its early days the club seems to have witnessed quite a lot of good humoured horseplay. In 1907 two young bachelors unyoked a bullock from a "bandy" (the principal means of transportation in those days), and let it loose in the ballroom causing the ladies to climb the pillars! In another incident, a somewhat boorish and unpopular member was tethered to a post, in the racquet court, together with a couple of donkeys for a whole night, in the belief that it might improve his manners. The present membership is of a much more phlegmatic disposition.'

I am, of course, talking of times when life in the tea garden was organised and comfortable. The early British pioneers had to go through tremendous hardships when they established the tea gardens in the mid-1800s. The journey from Calcutta to the tea districts in Assam would take over two months by paddle steamer up the Brahmaputra and then by country boats on its tributaries.

J Wetherstone in his splendid book *The Pioneers* quotes a planter's description of his arrival in Dibrugarh, in north-east Assam, to open up 300 acres of jungle in 1877 which graphically records the conditions under which planters worked. 'The preliminary arrangements consisted of selecting the area to be cleared, provisions for certain labour to do the work and provisions for 40 maunds of tea seeds, which was already on the way. My hut had only just been finished before I arrived, and the furniture consisted of boxes. One box served as a table, another as a chair, and third as a sideboard, and so on. The hut was small, its walls consisted of sun-dried thatched grass, fastened to a bamboo frame. A small window and door was made of the same materials. The roof was large, made of broad jungle leaves roughly sewn together, and I found it absolutely waterproof. The mud floor was covered with rice sacks, a thoughtful provision of the apothecary (Doctor Babu) to keep the damp from the master's feet.

After a rough meal I got to bed comfortably enough, but not so the cook, who made his bed on some boxes which were not too well balanced. A big log fire was kept going throughout the night, for wild beasts seemed to resent this clearing away of their natural home, and without a fire, which all beasts dislike, anything might have happened.'

The early planters lived lonely lives, as the gardens were far from each other. For lighting the long evenings there was nothing more than candles or kerosene lamps. The attitude of the local inhabitants was sometimes hostile and in flare-ups over the years, many planters and workers were killed. Tigers, leopards, wolves as well as snakes were a constant danger.

To quote a planter of the time, 'Assam was a dreadful place for tigers, and one had to be most careful as already two of the Company's assistants had been mauled on foot; a very dangerous game planting.' The death rate on the gardens was grim; cholera and dysentery took a heavy toll of both the planters and garden labourers. The young assistants, who went to the Assam jungles in those days, were told that there could be no return for five years. It would have been better to add the three words, 'If at all.'

Recreation for planters in the early pioneering days was rare – the day-to-day survival seemed to have been a full-time job. However, as the decades passed and life became more organised and gardens were successfully established, planters got together for cricket. They also played polo occasionally. The local inhabitants in Manipur had played polo for centuries and often the planters' team was coached by Manipur players. Hunting and shooting were popular pastimes. Bagging a tiger or a wild buffalo was everyone's ambition and it provided an exciting though dangerous sport. However, killing of tigers and elephants in the early days was so indiscriminate that the number of these wild animals in Assam was greatly reduced.

Talking of recreation, there were, of course, some mighty carousers among planters. It has been said that 'in some cases where time and weather had totally destroyed the rude huts in which the planters lived, the only indication of their original sites were the mounds of empty bottles left behind'. Somerset Maugham has, of course, immortalised the characters and the colourful lives on the estates.

Returning to the present and the technical aspects of processing the leaves, the tea estate factory is usually a large three- or four-storey building. The leaves from the pluckers' baskets are brought here for processing. In the factory, unlike the tea gardens, men do most of the work. Labourers and technicians wearing shorts bustle in the din and heat of the machinery.

The first stage of processing is withering, which is carried out by spreading the green leaves evenly on racks. They are left for eight to 24 hours during which time the leaves lose moisture and become flaccid. They are next brought down and fed into the rolling machines. These are large metal cylinders which rotate and assist in breaking and twisting the leaves inside the rollers. This releases the leaves' natural juices and enzymes and they begin to change colour, releasing a fresh and tangy apple-like smell that so pleasantly surrounds a tea factory. They leave the rollers in warm, twisted lumps and then these are fed into coarse sieves to be cooled and broken up. The sieves, known as roll-breakers, have a shaking and sifting action. The fine, tender leaves known as first quality come through the sieve first and are removed. The remaining leaves are re-rolled and again put on the roll-breakers, the process being repeated many times to produce, second, third and fourth qualities. Each quality is kept separate in the subsequent stages of processing.

The next stage is oxidisation, more commonly known as fermentation, where the leaves absorb oxygen. In the fermenting room the different qualities are thinly spread on trays in a cool humid atmosphere. This process which may take up to three hours gives tea its bright copper colour and also its characteristic flavour and aroma. The crucial fermentation process remains something of a mystery. No one knows exactly what alchemy produces the flavours, for certain cellular reactions during fermentation have never been fully understood or even identified.

The drying or the firing stage follows. The leaves are put on moving trays in a large drying chamber, through which a continuous blast of hot air is forced. This takes about half an hour and stops further oxidisation, after which the tea is fit for drinking.

The CTC or the Crush, Tear and Curl process of manufacture is similar to the orthodox tea making except for the rolling stage. For Crush, Tear, Curl manufacture the rolling is much more severe. Two cylinders, with only marginal clearance between them, move in inverse directions. This not only reduces the leaf size, but also ruptures the leaf cells and results in an accelerated and more intensive fermentation. In CTC tea, the liquor is thicker and it yields many more cups of tea per kilogram. The appearance of the dry leaf is granulated and it is black-brown in colour.

There are three main types of tea, but they all come from the same plant and their difference is one of manufacture and not of cultivation. The bulk of the tea is what is known as black tea. This goes through a full fermentation or oxidisation process. Green tea is unfermented, the leaves do not undergo any oxidisation. Oolong tea is semi oxidised. It is a speciality of Taiwan and has some of the characteristics of both black and green tea.

Green tea is still grown by the Chinese and Japanese for their own consumption. It is also grown in the Kangra Valley in north India, from where it goes to Kashmir where green tea is preferred. Elsewhere it is virtually unknown outside oriental restaurants. Green tea was much prized in China, and some teas had jasmine, gardenia, orange blossom and magnolia added for fragrance. The teas were put into chests, and freshly plucked flowers were strewn over every two-inch layer. The next day the mixture was poured on trays and toasted for a couple of hours and repacked into chests, with or without the flowers sifted out. The Chinese also had speciality black tea scented with lichee, rose and tangerine. But one that was the most exotic was known as Fragrance of a Young Girl tea. It is believed that this tea was made from the tiniest young buds just off the shoot, and then sold in small baskets worn over the breasts of young girls who sat in the shops as a merchandising aid. The warmth of their breasts matured the leaves. Perhaps this tea as well as the story, is best taken with a pinch of salt!

However, getting back to the mundane matter of manufacture of tea, the leaves, which were originally separated in the sifting stage, are now sorted into different sizes known as leaf, brokens, fannings and dust. The leaf grade is the largest in size, brokens next and the fannings are even smaller. Dust, sifted from both the brokens and fannings, is the smallest grade produced, and is strong, quick-infusing tea. Along with fannings it is widely used in tea bags. Contrary to popular belief dust can be of the first-quality and give an excellent cup of tea. Terms like Orange Pekoe, Flowery Orange Pekoe, Pekoe and Pekoe Souchong, although picturesque, only denote a certain size or appearance of leaf and have no reference to quality.

After sorting, each grade of tea is packed into aluminum-lined wooden chests. These chests preserve its freshness, prevent taints and make for easy storage and transportation.

Most of the managers and assistants on plantations today are Indians. Conditions have also changed and plantation management is quite different from the early days. There is a story of a superintendent in the 1930s who inspected a new English assistant's bungalow and quietly noted that the bookshelves were empty. There was not a single book. Nodding approvingly, he commented, 'That's good! Nothing to take your mind off your work.' But the view is changing from 'give me only public school boys', to 'give me graduates with intelligence', to 'give me agricultural science graduates'. It is realised that a more professional approach is necessary in plantation management and specialised knowledge in the practice of farming or planting, production, finance and marketing of garden produce is now desirable. Is the old planter heading for extinction to be replaced by 'businessmen in khaki shorts'? If the latter, he still must be the type who is ready to get mud on his boots and manage a large labour force and establish relationships with his workers.

In this context, it is worth mentioning the views of a former chairman of the Tea Board at a seminar at Calcutta in the early 1980s who visualised a picture of a typical group of tea gardens in the near future. 'The group,' he predicted, 'would have a central office, fully equipped with computerised systems. The managers in the gardens would be aided by instrumental techniques in cultivation, manufacturing and tasting. The field supervisors would be mobile on powered two wheelers and have available immediate communications with factory and office. The factories would be streamlined, largely automated and environmentally controlled.'

I believe in some instances his predictions have already been overtaken by events. Some older fashioned planters might growl, 'This sort of nonsense is not on, eggheads cannot produce tea.' But those days are gone. Companies now are not mollycoddled by a colonial government, but have to stand on their own two feet and face up to competition.

8

Tea Tasting and Blending

$f$rom the gardens, tea is packed in chests and sent to auction centres. Some of these centres are located within the country while others cater to the world markets. In India, the packed tea chests are sent to the auction centres in Calcutta, Guwahati in Assam, Cochin in Kerala and Conoor in the Nilgiri Mountains. In Sri Lanka, the auction centre is Colombo, in Bangladesh it is Chittagong, and in Indonesia it is Jakarta. In Africa, packed teas are sent to Nairobi and Mombasa for auctioning. Some gardens may, however, consign the teas directly to the oldest auction centre in London. Amsterdam is yet another market in Europe.

The gardens could sell their tea to private buyers, but the bulk of the world's teas are sold by public auction. Multinational tea companies like Brooke Bond (now part of Unilever) own not only tea plantation companies in

India, Sri Lanka and Africa but also separate companies, which pack, blend and market tea. But here also private sales by these plantation companies to the separate packet tea companies in the same group are limited, and the plantation companies send the bulk of their tea to public auctions to realise the best prices.

Tea is an internationally traded commodity. Therefore, the price paid by the packet tea companies and, ultimately, by the consumer is basically determined by the world demand and supply, both of tea as a whole and of teas of different types and qualities. Tea is a perishable commodity and cannot be stored overlong. Consequently, if the world demand is for the time being running ahead of supply the consumer may, to his or her dismay, find that tea prices are going up. If, on the other hand, the consumer finds that the prices are going down, it will be because supply is temporarily ahead of demand.

The procedure for the auction is virtually the same whether in Calcutta, Colombo or London. When the tea arrives from the gardens, it is stored in bonded warehouses. The brokers then inspect the tea, taste samples and value it. Full particulars are printed in the brokers' sale catalogue. The prospective buyers, who are generally the packet tea companies, consider the brokers' idea of the likely price but, naturally, are not over-influenced by their indications. They in turn draw their own samples of tea, taste them and make their own valuation before the sale. After this they decide which teas they are going to bid for. The senior tasters and blenders of the big tea companies are very highly paid men. As a result of astute buying and anticipation of market movement these senior tasters can make huge profits for the blending and packing companies.

Tea tasters, as experts in their field, require years of training. The palate and nose of the tea taster are as sensitively tuned as those of the wine expert and just as carefully nursed. Tea tasters estimate the value of the tea not only by tasting the liquor, but also by examining the dry leaf and infused leaf by sight, touch and by smell. Tasting is largely a matter of comparison, and it is essential when tasting a number of teas together, for each one to be brewed in the same way: an equal weight of tea; an equal quantity of boiled water; equal time for brewing – about five or six minutes; and equal size and style of pot and bowl. The amount of tea measured and weighed is governed by the size of the pot; in London the weight of a sixpence was used, while Brooke Bond traditionally used an old shilling or 5.65 grams. In India, the coin used to be a silver four-anna piece or a quarter *tola* (2.9 grams). Teas are usually tasted with milk because the colour can be better assessed with milk, and in any case consumers generally drink their tea with milk.

Samples for tasting are prepared in white porcelain pots with lids. The correct amount of tea having been weighed into each pot, water is brought to the boil and added as quickly as possible, filling each pot, which is then covered with a lid. After the infusion is completed, the pot is tipped so that the liquid drains off between the pot and lid into the bowl. A white porcelain bowl is used as white best reveals the colour of the tea. The infused leaf is tipped on to the reversed side of the lid and placed on top of the pot. This means that the bowl is now full of tea and the infused and dry leaf are ready for examination. Thus the infused tea or liquor, the infused leaf and the dry leaf are all ready displayed for the taster. He then proceeds to examine the dry leaf and inspects and smells the infused leaf. He takes a spoonful from the bowl and with a loud slurping noise takes the tea into his mouth, the inhalation drawing a fine spray against the taster's palate and wafting the aroma up the nasal passage. The liquor must not be too hot or the flavour cannot be accurately gauged. The tea is swilled around the mouth for two or three seconds in which time the taster's palate has completely registered the tea quality in comparison with innumerable other tastes that are stored up in his mind. He then somewhat irreverently spits it out into a big spittoon on wheels.

In the few seconds that the liquor is in his month, the taster registers how strong and brisk it is. Strength is thickness while briskness is a property of a good tea, which will keep well. The taster also judges the finer aspects of the liquor. Character is the distinctive taste, which depends upon the area in which tea is grown. Quality is aroma, which is found in abundance only during certain seasons of the year when leaf growth is slow. Flavour or bouquet is the ultimate in tea liquor and, being rare, is keenly sought after.

As some blends may require a mix of 20 or 30 teas from different gardens in different countries, tasters may sample 500 to 800 teas a day. This would represent about 30,000 to 40,000 chests.

The taster's description of tea in India used to contain over 100 terms, but many of these are now considered superfluous. Simpler descriptions are now preferred. Good quality dry leaf should be clear, even and well made. The infused leaf should be bright (the colour of copper) and not dull, green or uneven. The liquor should also be bright and not dull, aromatic and pungent, malty or full in taste. Certain second-flush Assam teas are known as greenfly, for at this time of the year, as the name implies, the bushes are attacked by greenflies. But, surprisingly enough, these insects give the tea an unusual but attractive flavour!

It is interesting to note that the liquoring qualities of coffee and of wines resemble those of teas, and the tasters of these commodities use many of the same expressions as tea tasters.

Good tasters can easily distinguish between Assam teas from north-east India with their thick body and strong malty taste; and Darjeelings from the foothills of the Himalaya with their fine quality and distinctive blackcurrant and muscatel flavour; south Indian teas from the Nilgiris with their distinct aroma and the high-grown teas from Sri Lanka with their fragrance and rich golden colour and the Indonesian teas somewhat similar to those from corresponding elevations in south India and Sri Lanka.

Mincing Lane had been the home of the London tea auctions for 160 years. The last auction here was held on June 29, 1998. This was 311 years after the East India Company first started auctioning tea at various locations in London, with Mincing Lane being the last. It became necessary to close down the London auctions as the volume of tea at the producer countries' own auctions increased enormously and little tea was sent for auctioning in London. The Calcutta auctions were started in 1861 while Colombo auctions commenced in 1883, Cochin in 1948, Chittagong in 1949, Conoor in 1963, Mombasa in 1969 and so on.

In most centres the auction halls are large and impressive with raised seating. (However, Conoor in the Nilgiris, which had newly been established as an auction centre, must have been an exception, as there was obvious improvisation and the auction was held in the Conoor Club lounge conveniently placed right next to the main bar, to which all hastily repaired at the conclusion!) The auction is conducted by a senior member of the broking company. He does not indulge in any eulogy of each lot as it comes up for sale – just the description, so many chests of such and such type of tea. The auction proceeds with speed and order and the bids come in so fast that for a layman it can be difficult to pick out the prices offered. As soon as a buyer has outbid his competitors the broker declares the tea sold. Despite the rapid bidding, during the winter months when there are large offerings from north India, the auction may carry on till late in the evenings.

For the buyers who have bought in bulk at the auctions, the next stage is blending of different teas in order to maintain the consistent quality and flavour of each blend. Teas from individual gardens vary not only throughout the season, but also from one season to the next due to local climatic conditions and also due to differences in manufacture. By blending the teas, the companies can create blends which maintain a constant quality. However, after the basic requirements of colour, strength and flavour of the blend have been met, the taster may find that the blend is averaging out at too high a price and to counteract this, quantities of tea are added known as fillers (these bring down the price without damaging the character of the blend). These fillers are available in international markets, from the peripheral districts of north India and Africa, the low-grown teas from Sri Lanka and tea from Indonesia and Argentina. However, in India with its 10,000 tea plantations producing over 1,000 varieties, which include fine, medium and low grades, blending can easily be done with indigenous teas.

It is only rarely that pure tea from an individual garden is marketed. This is for reasons of consistency in quality and the price factor discussed above. When a tea is labelled Darjeeling or Darjeeling blend, it may well be made up of 5 or 7 per cent pure Darjeeling with the rest comprising price reducers – medium quality or even low-quality teas which nevertheless achieve a pure Darjeeling flavour.

It is vital to know which teas blend together. Particular care has to be taken with teas of fine quality. It would, for instance, not be sensible to blend a fine Assam with a fine Sri Lankan tea as it would only mean that one would detract from the other – blends must have the pronounced flavour of one of the main growths only.

After the blending process has been completed by the tea tasters, the blending papers are passed on to the packing factories so that blending and packing on a mass scale can begin. Modern tea blending and packing factories are highly automated. Processes have been streamlined to reduce manual handling to a minimum. The tea chests from the gardens travel on an automatic conveyor to a de-lidder where the bottom of each chest is removed by mechanical saws. The chest is then emptied and the tea is put through dust extractors. It is next automatically lifted to a blending tower passing through a system of screens and magnets to remove wood chippings or any piece of metal or nails, which may have come from the tea chests. It is then rotated in huge drums, the capacity of which can be as much as 5,000 kilograms. This process mixes the different qualities and types of tea as required for the blend. The blended tea is next metered through automatic weighers and on to packing machines, which perform many complex operations at great speed, transforming paper, polythene, foil, etc., into lined packets or cartons. The tea packets are then ready for despatch and sales to retailers and, ultimately, to the consumers.

If tea is required to be packed in tea bags, separate machines not only form tea bags and fill them with tea, but also collate and pack them into preformed cartons.

9

Marketing of Tea

*M*arketing of tea could mean two things. First, there is the disposal of tea from the estates in bulk through the auctions or through private sale. Second, the marketing of tea in its branded packaged form to the consumer through the wholesale and retail network.

Since the first chest of tea landed in England, the retailers sold it in its loose form by weight. However, adulteration was always a danger and this became widespread, leaving the consumer at the mercy of unscrupulous operators who adulterated the tea. The next great innovation and the remedy against adulteration was provided by John Horniman about 1826 when he began selling tea in hygienically sealed, foil-lined paper packets. These were not only guaranteed unadulterated but also contained a uniformly weighed quantity of tea. We take packaging for granted today, but it was then an original concept. However, Horniman's venture was a small one and even after he started packaging, retailers continued to mix tea in the presence of their customers who would taste the tea until they were satisfied. Other customers bought tea from original chests and mixed it themselves.

The credit for packaging and marketing tea on a large scale must, therefore, go to Arthur Brooke in 1869. This was followed by Lyons, Lipton and Typhoo, who later joined Brooke Bond on grocers' shelves in England. Gradually, packet teas out-stripped and vanquished loose tea sales and grocers started stocking only branded packaged tea.

Arthur Brooke, as a 4-year-old, was reported to have often hitched a ride in a big wheelbarrow in which packets of tea from his father's shop were delivered around the neighbourhood. In 1869, as a young man, he set up a shop on his own and named it: Brooke Bond and Company. Who was Mr Bond? There was no one, the name was added because 'it seemed to sound well'. He used Brooke Bond as a trademark and today, over 130 years later, it continues to be used as such. It is, in fact, the largest-selling umbrella brand name in the world of tea.

Arthur Brooke built up his business through judicious buying of tea, good blending that appealed to consumer tastes, and creative advertising. By the 1890s, the business in Britain was prospering. Distribution was seen by Brooke to be the key to further successful expansion. As early as 1899, when motor vehicles were a rare thing, the company ordered one for deliveries but since it broke down every mile or so it was abandoned. Soon after, a fleet of horse-drawn vans were delivering stocks to retailers in several towns of the country and the system was gradually extended. D. Wainwright in his book *Brooke*

Bond, A Hundred Years, said, 'Some of the horses became legendary. One was said to have belonged to an undertaker, and if a funeral procession passed when the horse was standing outside a shop it would add the Brooke Bond van on to the cortege and have to be retrieved from the local cemetery. Another horse had once pulled a tram, and would only stop at one ding of a bell, and start again at two.' By the 1920s, the horse-drawn vans were replaced by the well-known little red motor vans. There were several hundreds of these vans of Trojan make. The van had two-inch solid tyres and non-detachable wheels. It had only two controls, and a primitive handle which had to be cranked by hand for it to start. So the salesman soon learnt to park it wherever possible on the tops of hills. In 1924, a salesman was once summoned for driving at 18 m.p.h. in Sheffield. The speed limit for solid tyred vehicles was 15 m.p.h., but defence counsel proved that the hollow tube inside the solid rubber formed a vacuum and the tyre was not solid. The case was dismissed.

Arthur Brooke laid the foundations of a tea business that was to span close to one hundred countries and become a worldwide multinational. It is remarkable that this great business grew out of a single retail shop. The group is comprised of plantation companies in India, Sri Lanka and Africa as well as packet tea manufacturing and marketing companies in a large number of countries. It also has interests in coffee, corned beef, soup cubes and spices and owns cattle ranches in South America and Zimbabwe.

The Brookes were a charming family. John and David Brooke had that personal touch which is so sadly lacking in the modern day corporate culture. I remember one particular visit as a young man to the UK for a short

conference where the wives had not been invited.
However, my wife made her private arrangements and
accompanied me against the advice of some local
colleagues. When John Brooke, the chairman of the
group, heard that she was also in London, he was very
considerate and asked how we were faring as the Indian
Government was very stringent with the release of foreign
exchange at that time. I do not recall my answer, but it
must have been effective enough because that same
afternoon, I received a large wad of sterling notes with
the compliments of the chairman. This enabled us to
have a splendid holiday in Italy. Company rules were not
rigid enough to interfere with the human touch. John
and David Brooke were multi-millionaires but their lives
were simple and unostentatious. Their main interest in
life was their business and the people in it.

Marketing of tea in India in its branded-packaged form
may best be illustrated by a look at Brooke Bond India
Limited, which was the largest company in the group.
While the marketing of tea does not differ greatly from
the marketing of any other consumer product, some
aspects of Brooke Bond India's marketing particularly in
the rural areas does set it apart.

With increasing prosperity, the consumption of tea in
India had increased significantly, and by the 1970s the
country had become the largest consumer of tea in the
world with an annual consumption of 400 million
kilograms. It had thus out-stripped the United Kingdom
as the world's largest tea-drinking nation. This was,
obviously, in terms of total consumption and not per
capita consumption.

By this time, Brooke Bond India Limited had also
grown into the largest packet tea company in the world.

Within India it was ranked as the fifth largest public limited company in terms of turnover (*India Today*, May 16-31, 1979).

The Indian Company was started in a small way by J.R.F. McKay, a Scotsman, in 1901 at Calcutta. Several brands of packet tea were launched – McKay must have had a penchant for colours – for he named them Red, Green, Black and even Violet label. Another brand launched later was called Kora, as McKay mistakenly believed that kora meant pure in Hindi. However, despite the word's association with blank or unwashed, the brand thrived and then grew! Packaging of tea was in square and round tins, which would be impossibly costly today. Several years later, cartons, paper foil packets and much later, paper poly laminates appeared in the market.

Seventy years on, Brooke Bond India became the world's number one packet tea company. It had seven factories located strategically all over the country, 34 sales offices and more than 10,000 employees. Its only competitor was Lipton India although the latter's sales were only half those of Brooke Bond India's.

Part of the credit for the huge expansion in the sales of tea, in India, must go to the pioneering efforts of these two companies, who with the extensive retail distribution of their packet tea, made it available to the consumer not only in the urban areas but more importantly in the rural areas. Interestingly, however, loose tea, which as the term implies is sold loose to the consumer by weight, easily outsold the combined sales of the two packet tea companies. This was essentially because loose tea was cheaper and of a reasonable quality.

The retail distribution system of Brooke Bond India deserves a brief discussion because it was unique. The company's sales force of almost 3,000 men supplied tea every week in the towns and every fortnight in the villages directly to a colossal 750,000 retailers spread over 27,000 towns and villages. And contrary to general trade practice, the retailers paid cash for the company's products. Brooke Bond did not use stockists or wholesalers as other companies did. Instead, stock was delivered to retailers through a network of 2,000 company depots located all over the country. The company could thus deliver their stock to all these towns and villages from the Himalaya in the north to Cape Comorin in the south, a distance of about 3,000 kilometres, and from the Burma border in the east to the Arabian Sea in the west, which is about the same distance.

The 27,000 towns and villages may sound like a large number, but when one relates this to the fact that the country has 600,000 towns and villages, one starts to wonder! However, it must be appreciated that the majority of these villages are very remote, they do not have an all-weather road and some do not have electricity. Consequently, it is necessary to be selective in the coverage of villages, more so as costs mount up faster the further one physically takes one's stock into inaccessible rural areas. This is not only because distances are greater and roads are poor, but also because a truck or any alternative mode of transport used for delivery does not find any loads to carry back to base, further escalating cost. Thus in the selection of villages, the company identified the feeder villages or the ones from which the local wholesaler could channel the stock further down to yet smaller villages.

This sales coverage of towns and villages took the company far beyond the facilities of rail or road transport and the banking system. Not only did the sales force of 3,000 men, therefore, carry stock on motor vans but also on bicycles, horses and bullock carts, boats on the rivers, camels in the deserts and mules on the mountains – a great deal of innovation in transport was necessary.

The Brooke Bond system of distribution was extremely efficient. It was probably the largest direct distribution network in the world. However, while it could be viable up to the 1970s when the wages of the sales force and cost of transport were modest, this scenario was changing and with increasing costs the system became increasingly more expensive and ultimately non-viable.

A change-over from direct retail distribution to the wholesale channels of distribution became inevitable. In India, there is a well-developed trading framework based on the wholesale and retail network. This has developed over the centuries thanks to the *banyias* who represent a unique hereditary trading caste. As the company's direct retail distribution became uneconomic, it fell back on this traditional distribution network and appointed stockists and wholesalers thus cutting down on manpower as well as freight costs.

The Indian market covers a vast spectrum of consumers across the socio-economic scale ranging from the urban rich to the rural poor. In order to match this spread, Brooke Bond India launched ten brands of tea, each brand having packets of seven or eight different sizes, making a total of 70 or 80 packs. The more affluent consumers buy the large pack sizes of the more expensive brands, while consumers lower down the socio-economic scale buy the cheaper brands and smaller pack sizes. Contrast this with the United Kingdom where the different brands have only one pack size – the quarter pound (110 grams). The most interesting Indian packs were what were called paise packets, which contained only two or three grams of tea – enough to make two cups. In the 1970s, this packet sold for 5 paise though, of course, later it was priced at 50 paise and more. The paise packets were ideal for the daily wage workers, who lived on their day-to-day earnings and bought their requirements every day. These extraordinary packs were the smallest and cheapest branded and packaged consumer product in the world. The company sold 240 million of these envelope packs every month, mainly in the rural areas, and they represented one-fifth of the company's tea turnover. The paise packets were a very good example of what can be termed as barefoot marketing.

India is a vast country with people of different racial, cultural and historical backgrounds. Each state is like a huge market in itself. Prosperity differs from state to state. Therefore, marketers must have a sound idea about regional attitudes, habits and social standards. While the urban population in the different areas of the country are more homogenous, the rural population continues to cling to their regional tastes and characteristics. This highlights the need for intensive market research. Taking this into account, the company had regional brands tailored to regional preferences and supported by regional advertising campaigns. This is in sharp contrast to current theories relating to international brand names supported by globalised advertising campaigns ignoring the diversity of backgrounds, cultures and economic status. Even the models are foreigners, which sets up a mental and emotional resistance straight away. In any case, the taste of the pudding is in the eating – and Brooke Bond India's regional and statewise approach was admirably successful.

With a vital 50 per cent of the company sales coming from the rural areas, advertising in the villages became crucially important. While in the urban areas there are multiple advertising media available, in the rural areas such media are limited. Television did not then have the reach, and adult illiteracy restricted press advertising. Therefore, Brooke Bond developed some unconventional media for communication and advertising. There were the propaganda motor vans, equipped with microphones and cinema equipment, which visited villages on a regular basis showing advertising films and offering gifts against purchase of tea. Company representatives also participated in the colourful village fairs and festivals, which are an essential part of village life, and where they set up company stalls for propaganda and selling. Thousands of hoardings and wall signs were also put up in the villages. As most painters of such hoardings were recruited locally, the paintwork was not always of the highest order. On one occasion this led to some embarrassment for the product manager concerned. Unfortunately for him, a company director happened to see one of the hoardings on which the woman enjoying a cup of tea was badly painted and looked like an over made-up prostitute. The next day the product manager received a short note from the director, which read 'while passing the village of Sumerkheri, I saw your Red Label WHORDING'.

Another interesting medium utilised was touring cinemas, which showed feature films in villages (either outdoors or by setting up tents). There were a couple of thousand such touring cinemas in the country, and Brooke Bond used several hundreds to show their advertising films.

Two basic guidelines had to be kept in mind while developing advertising for the rural areas. We have touched upon the heterogeneity of consumers in the rural areas. Thus rural advertising campaigns had to be more regional in appeal. A national campaign .with a national theme, while fine for the urban markets, would not have the same impact in the rural areas.

Second, for a rural audience Brooke Bond insisted on advertising which was simple in presentation and could be comprehended by the villagers. It was felt that the villagers should be able to associate with the images and visuals through which advertising was trying to reach them. No innovations were required here: they would be lost in the novelty and the message might escape them. In the urban areas there already exists a community consciousness of products and brand reputations have grown through generations, but in the rural areas there existed a first generation buyer for whom there was no frame of reference. Advertising and promotion, therefore, had to be understood before it could either convince or motivate.

Brooke Bond, the British parent company, was taken over by Unilever, the giant Anglo-Dutch multinational, in 1985. The takeover was bitterly opposed by the Brooke Bond London Board. But in a fortnight, Unilever purchased the majority shares of the company on the London Stock Exchange and took over control. Accordingly, Brooke Bond India became part of the Unilever group. Interestingly, the merger of Brooke Bond India with their main competitor Lipton India followed this, as the latter had been earlier absorbed by Unilever. Brooke Bond Lipton India Limited thus became an even more formidable force holding a major share of the packet tea market. In more recent times, the various Unilever companies in India have been merged and have now become Hindustan Lever Limited.

10

Tea Miscellanea

*I*t does now seem astonishing that in Europe before the advent of tea and coffee the only alternatives to water were alcohol and milk. Much the same was true of India and the neighbouring countries, except that sherbet and fresh fruit juices have always played a considerable part here. Today, of course, there is a plethora of drinks, which directly or indirectly challenge the supremacy of tea and coffee all over the world.

Whatever the competition, it will not be easy to dislodge tea: tea is a habit not only because of its pleasant taste but also because it is refreshing. On a cold winter day or a hot summer day tea is equally welcome, for it is a warming drink and through its ability to stimulate the blood vessels a cooling drink as well.

The medical profession has done much study on tea, its pharmacology, and its effect on health. According to the study, the main stimulants in tea are caffeine and tannin. The caffeine content is four per cent by weight in the leaf. When tea is drunk the warmth of the drink is at once felt, but the stimulus due to the caffeine comes about a quarter of an hour later. It is thus the ideal reviver with a long-lasting effect. Coffee contains two per cent caffeine by weight in the leaf, and its stimulating effect is quicker than tea but it does not last as long.

The tannin in the tea should not be confused with tannic acid, which would be harmful for digestion and has been ignorantly associated with tea. Tannin gives tea its pungency and much of its taste. Many beverages contain tannin and a cup of cocoa contains considerably more tannin than a cup of tea.

The combination of caffeine and tannin in a cup of tea is a happy one as it gives both an immediate and a delayed lift without inducing secondary depressing effects. Thus tea is as good an agent for relieving fatigue as has yet been found; it increases speed and clarity of thought.

The doctors go on to add that tea is beneficial at all times of the day, but particularly on waking up and after meals. Together with the milk in it, it has a buffering action on the stomach acids which have been collecting during sleep. It takes the heaviness out of a meal by promoting peristalsis (getting the intestinal muscles moving). There are also certain enzymes in tea which promote digestion. Another effect of tea is to inhibit the action of the vagus nerve, which causes stomach glands to overproduce acid when one is anxious or excited. Therefore, tea is, both reviving and soothing. Recent research suggests that tea also has important antioxidant properties that help ward off heart diseases.

Thus modern medicine fully vindicates the belief in the virtue of tea held by tea drinkers for over 2,000 years. But tea is not a medicine and not drunk as a remedy for illness.

* * *

England was one of the earliest countries in Europe to take to tea drinking. Tea, here, was initially served in coffee houses, the first of which was established in Oxford in 1650. By the early 1700s, coffee houses had become very popular, especially in London, and there were 500 of them in the area now known as the West End. They became the centre of London's social life. Businessmen and merchants frequented them to negotiate deals. The intelligentsia came in large numbers to discuss literary matters and politics. Yet others went to coffee houses simply to relax. Lloyds, which first started as a coffee house, and specialised in purveying the latest shipping news, became the greatest insurance centre in the world. Policy brokers of the 17th century, seeking subscribers, found Lloyds invaluable as many prospective clients frequented it. However, the government started to view coffee houses with suspicion, for the gossip was dangerous and political discussion seditious. They were considered such dens of iniquity that in 1675 Charles II issued a proclamation for the suppression of coffee houses, but was later forced to withdraw it, in view of the public outcry against it. Coffee houses remained popular for almost a hundred years after that and tea drinking continued to be promoted by them. By the 1750s, however, the heyday of coffee houses had ended partially because their role was taken over by clubs and also because they were purely a male preserve.

Apparently it was in the old coffee houses that the practice of tipping was born – customers would toss a coin into a box marked T.I.P. (To Insure Promptness). The practice is a veritable scourge today in western countries.

Meanwhile, tea had moved into homes and was drunk mainly in the afternoon. The huge quantities of tea being imported into Britain suggested that tea was being drunk by millions of people, but curiously 'without their inventing afternoon tea'. Most literature on tea gives credit to a Duchess of Bedford for establishing the institution of afternoon tea, serving cakes, and other goodies with the tea. It proved hugely popular because it was customary in England, at the time, to have a substantial breakfast, a lunch of little account and dinner served later in the evening. The long hours between breakfast and dinner left many a stomach protesting and afternoon tea as a meal proved irresistible. The Duchess' innovation became a fashion. But then afternoon tea had already developed as an institution in the homes and was an occasion not for dressing up and making social conversation, but rather for relaxing and being comfortable in one's own living room.

The tea gardens of London also did much to establish tea as a social beverage. By the late 1700s, there were several tea gardens in the city where both men and women with their children could enjoy the fairy lights, watch fireworks and eat masses of bread and butter with their tea, all to the accompaniment of live bands. The most famous tea gardens in London were Ranelagh, Vauxhall and Marylebone, patronised by men and women of fashion and even by Royalty. The admission charge, which included tea, bread and butter, was as much as half a crown. They had lantern-lit walks and music, and supper was served at an extra charge. Horace Walpole, Henry Fielding and Dr Johnson used to go to the tea gardens with their friends. People of other classes and humble wage earners enjoyed going to other tea gardens in suburban London. But, gradually, the tea gardens went downhill and the wholesome entertainment they provided was replaced by rowdyism. Gervas Huxley (*Talking of Tea*, 1956) said, 'Watchmen were employed to keep order and some gardens provided escorts to conduct parties home after dark. Nevertheless, pickpockets haunted many of the gardens and some of the female frequenters were certainly of dubious character. A correspondent reported how he was frequently accosted by women with the request, "Pray, sir, will you treat me with a dish of tea." The technique for making a lady's acquaintance was for the gentleman to tread on the lady's train, to apologise profusely and finally, to suggest tea in one of the arbours.' By about 1850, the vogue for tea gardens was over. 'The English lost their taste for open-air entertainment, although the French with their cafe concerts and the Germans with their beer gardens have continued their equivalent of English tea gardens.'

With afternoon tea and cakes becoming customary in homes and with the tea gardens disappearing, the next stage was inevitable and the English tea shop was born. The first was opened by Thomas Twining, then a young salesman for a London tea merchant. So far women were not admitted to the coffee houses but Twining opened his doors to them and this was hugely popular. Twining became a famous tea brand in later years and one that is well known even today. These tea shops proliferated fast and soon dotted the whole country. The best known of these were the Lyons tea shops, associated with

J. Lyons and Company. Its founder was impressed by
the difficulty of obtaining light refreshments anywhere
except in pubs and other licensed houses and decided to
enter the catering business. His first tea shop was opened
in 1894 at Piccadilly, London, and 'this made it possible
for the Victorian families of suburbia to come to London
town – hitherto there had been nowhere respectable for
Mama and the children to have a cup of tea or a midday
meal'. The Lyons tea shops soon increased in number
and became important in English social life. Deny
Forrest quotes a description of a Lyons tea shop at the
turn of the 19th century, '. . . in many respects very
different in appearance from the present version. The
white and gold fascia was much the same as now, but
red silk covered the walls and gas-lighted chandeliers
hung from the ceiling. You sat in a red plush chair and
were served by a very smart waitress in a grey uniform
with a voluminous skirt going down to the floor.'

Quite a difference from the unattractive plastic glasses
and pottery mugs in use in many places today. There
seems to be a class division here with the upper class still
using exquisite china, while lower down the social scale
a large mug is the norm.

* * *

The traditional tea ware of China had an important
influence on the development of such ware in Europe.
When Lu Yu wrote his classic on tea *Ch'a Ching* about
AD 800, there were no teapots and powdered tea was
infused in the teacup or bowl. Discerning tea drinkers,
however, insisted on taking their tea only in fine icy blue
porcelain cups, which showed the colour of the tea better.

Somewhat later, spouted pitchers used for wine inspired the development of teapots. The Ming period (14th and 15th centuries), which was notable for its porcelain and the development of coloured glazes that could protect the painting underneath, saw the rise to prominence of the Yi Hsing teapots. They became popular all over China and Japan. The Yi Hsing teapots were small in size so that each person could have a pot to himself and they had elegant lines and were of great beauty. Sometimes, however, they were stylised into not so beautiful creations like flowers, vegetables, animals and other weird shapes. The teapot of today has not changed in essentials from the Yi Hsing pot despite all efforts to improve upon it.

The earliest imports of tea into Europe also brought the Yi Hsing teapots and these were imitated all over the continent. Chinese porcelain with its magical translucence was a mystery to the Europeans and it was not until 1713 that the secret was unlocked and vitrified pottery with a white translucence was made at the Meissen factory in Germany. Teasets formed an important part of the early Meissen output. After 1745, the manufacture of porcelain began in England and the four famous porcelain makers, Chelsea, Bow, Derby and Worcester, began to make their beautiful tea ware. Chelsea was famous for its hexagonal teapots painted with Aesop's fables, Bow made barrel-shaped teapots and Derby melon-shaped ones. The variety of decoration on tea ware was considerable and it was all individually painted by hand.

Earthenware, which is coarse and opaque, and stoneware which is fine but not translucent also continued to be used for tea services.

In the early part of the 18th century, silver became the material for teasets. Elegant silver and plated tea services started reigning supreme. Teapots, milk jugs and sugar bowls exquisitely wrought in pear, spherical, and melon shapes started gracing tea tables.. It is said that some of the finest silverware ever made in England was about this time and it was tea that inspired it.

In the 19th century, Staffordshire developed bone china on the formula established by Josiah Spode II. This was a hybrid porcelain containing bone ash. The Staffordshire industry grew rapidly and bone china tea ware or 'tea equipage', as it was called at the time, flooded the world market. Later J. Wedgewood entered the scene and revolutionised the Staffordshire industry.

Chinese teacups were made of delicate porcelain and were without handles or saucers. Europeans initially followed this style and cups had no handles but the saucers were deep like a shallow bowl and the cooling tea was sometimes drunk directly from it. The Europeans later added two practical improvements – handles for cups and shallow saucers. With larger quantities of tea being quaffed, bigger cups also came into vogue. One style which deserves mention is described by Gervas Huxley, 'The late 19th century did, however, produce one ingenious teacup variant – the moustache cup. This cup was fitted with a bar across the inside, upon which the drooping moustache rested so that the tea could be swallowed without first being passed through a hirsute filter.'

* * *

The Indian *dhaba* or hot tea shop is unique. These *dhabas* are not only numerous in the towns and villages of the country, but are found every few miles flanking the national and state highways and also obscure country roads. Brooke Bond India had on its sales coverage about 300,000 of these, but my guess is that there must be well over a million of these hot tea shops in India. In the open countryside, the *dhabas* are spacious with seating outside as well as inside and festooned with colourful flags and merchandising material, but in the back alleys of cities they are mere holes in the wall. In Rajasthan, some country tea shops have stately elephants and gawky camels standing by to offer rides to customers – a splendid sales promotion.

Generally, two parts water, one part rich buffalo milk, the tea leaves and sugar are all put together into a kettle. This mixture is given two or three quick boils and poured from the kettle held high into glasses placed some distance below, so that it cools slightly and you can literally enjoy a yard of tea in each glass. The tea is aptly called *khada chamach* because it is so strong, sweet and thick that a spoon will stand upright! Truck drivers on the highways find that the stronger the tea the longer they can keep fatigue at bay.

One of the senior Brooke Bond tea tasters, an Englishman, accompanied a sales manager on a sales trip to gauge for himself the consumer reaction to the tea being blended by his department. After a longish drive in one of the company cars they stopped for a glass of tea at a village *dhaba*. A foreigner being a novelty in those parts was eyed with some curiosity. However, the tea arrived and the first sip foxed the taster; being a good tea taster he went into the familiar routine – took a spoon of tea and with a loud slurping sound took it into his mouth, swilled it for the regulation time and then spat it out. The *dhaba* owner viewed the whole process with consternation, but when his tea was rudely spat out he was most indignant and asked the sales manager, who happened to be an Indian, whether all *firangees* (foreigners) were crazy like the one with him. Explanations, as you can imagine, did not come easy.

In Gujarat, tea is usually drunk flavoured with cardamom or ginger. This is aptly known as masala tea and since the spice is dominant the quality of leaf is secondary. In Kashmir, only green tea is drunk and it is made in silver samovars or tinned copper ones and infused with ginger, cinnamon and cardamom.

The way tea is drunk in different parts of the world are myriad. The Russians, as old and ardent tea drinkers as the English, prepare a strong brew which serves as an essence. A small quantity of this essence is poured into a glass and hot water added from the always simmering samovar. Generous amount of sugar and a flavouring of lemon are added to the glass of tea. Sometimes a lump of sugar is kept in the month and the strong bitter tea is sipped through it. 'Ecstasy,' wrote Pushkin, 'is a glass full of tea and a piece of sugar in the mouth.'

Brick tea was drunk in Russia, China and Tibet till the late 19th century. The tea leaves were thoroughly pounded then shaped and pressed into moulds, dried over wood fire and formed into bricks. They were convenient to transport over long distances, especially when animals were used for this purpose.

In Tibet, the tea leaves are boiled for several hours till the infusion is black. A little salt is thrown in with a large piece of rancid yak butter and then the mixture is thoroughly churned. This hot-buttered tea is served in small wooden bowls. It does not sound appetising but the Tibetans enjoy 30 or 40 bowls a day of this concoction.

In Korea, tea is served with raw eggs. The eggs are sucked from the shells between sips of tea. The Burmese pickle their tea or steep it in oil. In Central Asia, the leaves are boiled in a tinned copper pot until the tea is very strong. Cream from goat's milk is added and while the tea is boiling tiny bits of bread are soaked in it.

* * *

Two American innovations are iced tea and tea bags. Iced tea started as a fortunate accident. At the World Fair in St Louis in 1904, the tea producers of India had dispatched a public relations man to try and propagate Indian tea, as most of the tea drunk in America at the time was Chinese. The mid-west summer of 1904 was unpleasantly hot and sultry, as usual, and there were few takers at the Fair for the steaming Indian tea. In desperation, on one hot day, the public relations man made samples of tea in glasses and put in plenty of ice. The cold refreshing drink was an immediate success and iced tea was born. It is still popular in the US as a hot weather beverage and even those who never drink hot tea find the iced version a good thirst quencher. It is usually taken with lemon or mint. However, cold tea has never really caught on anywhere else, perhaps because the flavoured iced version does not really taste like tea at all. Nevertheless, it is a very refreshing drink and is important in boosting American tea consumption. USA consumes five times as much coffee as tea-based beverages, but it is nevertheless the world's third largest importer of tea.

Tea bags, which appeared in America in the early 1900s, were also an accidental development when a New York importer decided to send his samples in hand stitched silk bags. Despite their use in the USA for several decades, tea bags did not cross the Atlantic till the 1950s. The appeal of tea bags is that they save time and labour. The consumer finds the disposal of the spent soggy tea leaves (as opposed to tea bags) in the cold pot difficult. They tend to clog the kitchen sink. If they are swilled down the toilet and flushed it seems uncivilised. They can be put in the flower beds in the garden, but with mixed results. One can, of course, 'bring them back to life with boiling water but then their vitality has vanished and you are drinking a ghost'.

Despite being labelled as yet another example of American vandalism, tea bags have forged ahead in Britain and hold a major share of the retail market. In the huge Indian market, tea bags have hardly made an impression in the domestic segment, but they do figure in hotels and other catering institutions, where portion control offered by tea bags is considered an advantage.

The connoisseur will always maintain that tea from tea bags is inferior to leaf tea and as one of them said, 'To prefer tea bags to real tea is to exalt the shadow over the substance.' The paper from which the tea bags are formed seems to impart a mild taint to the tea. In addition, tea bags are far more expensive than packet tea.

Another recent innovation is instant tea, produced from black tea by extracting the liquor from the processed leaves, concentrating the extract under low pressure and drying the concentrate to a powder by freeze drying, spray drying or vacuum drying. Low temperatures are used to minimise loss of flavour and aroma. The use of instant tea is mainly for vending machines and it has little appeal otherwise. It is unlikely to play a significant part in the near future.